The Asian Literature Bibliography Series

GUIDE TO JAPANESE DRAMA

**The Asian Literature Program
of the Asia Society**
General Editor

Guide to

JAPANESE DRAMA

LEONARD C. PRONKO

*895
62
PRONKO*

G. K. HALL & CO.
70 LINCOLN STREET, BOSTON, MASS.
1973

Library of Congress Cataloging in Publication Data
Pronko, Leonard Cabell.
  Guide to Japanese drama.

  (The Asian literature bibliography series)
  1. Japanese drama—Bibliography. I. Title.
II. Series.
  Z3308.L5P76   016.8956'2'008   73–8506
ISBN 0–8161–1108–1

To the teachers, administrators, and students of the Kabuki Training Program of the National Theatre of Japan, whose friendship, generosity and dedication permitted me to deepen my understanding of Japanese theatre.

Contents

FOREWORD

This annotated bibliography series on Asian literature was initiated in response to the needs of the nonspecialist. It is hoped that the summaries and evaluations to selected works available in translation together with the general introduction in each guide to the literature under examination will aid educators and students on both the secondary and college level as well as the general reader and those in institutions who want to build up responsibly their collection of Asian writings. Although compiled for an audience completely unfamiliar with Asian literature, these guides are also intended to be reference works for students and scholars exploring a particular subject. In addition, they should benefit those in disciplines other than literature—Asian heritage studies, anthropology, history, philosophy, the social sciences—who wish to take advantage of translated literature as a rich source of material for their studies. Books that are not available in libraries may be ordered through the publishers or through such specialized bookstores as Paragon Book Gallery, New York, Hutchins Oriental Books, California, or The Cellar Book Shop, Michigan.

Naturally, each author has his own criteria for the way the material in his guide is selected, presented, and judged. However, the intent of the author has been to indicate clearly and honestly the range and artistic merit of all the titles annotated and thereby guide the reader to those specific works which will satisfy his scholarly and aesthetic needs.

Arranged by topic and chronology, each guide covers the translated literature from the earliest times to today, but none pretend to be comprehensive. In most cases, works that are not recommended or have been superseded by better versions have been excluded. Omitted also are very specialized studies and inaccessible translations (thus excluding much of what has appeared in magazines and journals), and a number of translations which are too new to have been included in the guides. This increase in translation activities is a welcome sign. It points to a growing awareness of the importance of listening to Asian voices (rather than only to Western interpreters of Asia) and to the growing recognition of the place of Asian writings in world literature and of the place of translators in the creative field. Hopefully, these guides will serve the reader who later turns to translations not annotated or discussed here.

A series of this scope required the involvement of a number of people. I would especially like to thank the authors who have prepared these guides and the many scholars who have acted as consultants throughout the preparation of each manuscript, offering invaluable suggestions and criticism. Acknowledgment is also due Junnko Tozaki Haverlick of the Asian Literature Program of The Asia Society under whose editorial guidance these guides were prepared.

BONNIE R. CROWN, Director
Asian Literature Program

The Asia Society

NOTE TO THE READER

The Japanese names in this bibliography are given in their normal Japanese order, that is, family name first, followed by given name. Each play is generally referred to by the title which is given in the volume under discussion. Thus some plays are referred to by their translated titles, and others to their better-known romanized Japanese titles. Boldface numbers given in parentheses for cross-reference indicate entry numbers, not page numbers.

Japanese consonants are pronounced much as English consonants, with the exception of *f* which lies somewhere between English *f* and *h*, and *r* which resembles a Spanish single *r* with occasionally a shade of *l* in it. *G* in Japanese romanization is invariably pronounced hard (as in *gas*). The vowels are pure as in Spanish or Italian, although under certain circumstances *i* and *u* tend to neutralize or almost disappear.

Publishers and book dealers handling Japanese publications are to be found on the East and West coasts. The first two listed below are publishers and can supply their own publications. The others will order items by any Japanese publisher, or may have them in stock.

Charles E. Tuttle Company, 28 South Main Street, Rutland, Vermont 05701.

Kōdansha International, 599 College Avenue, Palo Alto, California 94306.

Paragon Book Gallery, Ltd., 14 East 38th Street, New York, N. Y. 10016.

Japan Publications Trading Company, Ltd., 1255 Howard Street, San Francisco, California 94103.

Kinokuniya Book Store of America Company, Ltd., Japanese Cultural and Trade Center, 1581 Webster Street, San Francisco, California 94115.

Hutchins Oriental Books, 1034 Mission Street, South Pasadena, California.

Orientalia Bookshop, Inc., 61 4th Avenue, New York, N. Y. 10003.

INTRODUCTION

The theatregoer in search of performances in any cosmopolitan center of the Western world may choose among plays in the avant-garde forms, realistic works of the modern era, or revivals of classics from the past presented, for the most part, in styles which have little connection with the traditions of bygone days. Or he may choose opera performances which prolong European traditions of the eighteenth and nineteenth centuries, ballet which largely lives on conventions of the past century, or nontheatrical musical forms which hark back to much earlier periods. In Tokyo, the same spectator would have all of these theatrical opportunities, and many more, representing a far broader spectrum because the Japanese, unlike most of us in the West, have not lost their old theatrical traditions as they absorbed new ones.

Alongside the underground experimental theatres, the most formless happenings, and outrageous concrete music, exist the staid nō theatres, the highly ritualistic court dances, and dozens of forms of traditional music. In one building, girlie shows are taking place on an upper floor at the same time that extravagant musical reviews go on below. Down the street, the all-girl Takarazuka presents operettas, reviews, and melodramas bringing together in a colorful extravaganza the most flamboyant elements of five centuries of Japanese entertainment along with Western melodrama, musical comedy, and the Folies Bergères. Just around the corner, a German opera company performs, or a Japanese troupe plays Giraudoux or Anouilh, while five blocks away the all-male kabuki theatre presents its ten-hour-long programs of dances and plays integrating all the theatre arts. In addition to these major theatrical entertainments, numerous peripheral ones are available as well: story-telling, sentimental soap operas, folk and festival entertainments.

The rich variety of theatre in Japan today can be ascribed, at least in part, to the paradoxical character of the nation; conservative on the one hand, on the other, it is curious and open-minded toward the new and the non-Japanese. The earliest form of entertainment, still represented among the performing arts of Japan, demonstrates both these tendencies. The music and dance of the Imperial Household, *gagaku* (elegant music) and *bugaku* (dance music), originated in the eighth century when music and dances from the Asian mainland (via China, but coming from as far as Tibet, India, and even Persia) were introduced at the court and blended with already existing forms. Curiously enough, whereas the originals on the Asian mainland died out over a thousand years ago, the Japanese forms, stylized and refined to the courtly tastes of the eighth to the eleventh centuries, have persisted until today and are performed on ceremonial occasions in the Imperial Palace in Tokyo, and in several shrines in the country. The strength of tradition has kept alive an art which, in its origins, was a foreign importation, but had by the tenth century already become a particularly Japanese art form.

Gagaku and bugaku are, despite their exotic derivation, in many ways typical of the courtly culture of the Heian period (782–1185). Chinese culture, along with Buddhism, had been introduced as early as the sixth century and the Imperial Court in the capital city of Heian (today's Kyoto)—the arbiter in all matters of taste and culture as well as the political center of the country—slowly assimilated the writing system, religion, architecture, and other marvels imported from the more ancient country to the west. With its careful symmetry, quiet dignity, and elegant ceremoniousness set off by elaborate and colorful costumes and sometimes masks, the bugaku seems a fitting representative of the aesthetic and ceremonious Heian society depicted in the first masterpiece of Japanese literature, *The Tale of Genji*. The image of the refined courtier—supposedly a poet, calligrapher, scholar and gentleman all in one, who fell in love sight unseen because of a beautifully written poem scented with the proper perfume—seems somehow appropriate for a society which relished the polished and graceful postures of the highly abstract bugaku with its subtly suggested themes emptied of dramatic content and emotion.

The hyperaestheticism of the Heian court was the outward manifestation of a crumbling within, and announced the doom of the effete nobility, dominated in the late Heian period by the Taira family of regents. The Taira subsequently engaged in a bitter battle with the Minamoto family and were exterminated by them during the thirty-year Gempei Wars. These wars, and the families engaged in them, furnish the subject matter for a number of literary works, as well as for numerous dramatic pieces belonging to a variety of theatrical forms.

The story of political power in Japan is one of slow descent from the emperor at the summit to his regents, and then down to the military dictators, known as shōgun, beginning with Minamoto Yoritomo in 1185. Yoritomo set up his capital in the frontier outpost of Kamakura, far from the cultural oasis of the emperor's residence in Heian, which remained the nominal capital. In succeeding centuries, although the shōgun's headquarters sometimes shifted back to Kyoto, the power did not revert to the emperor until the middle of the nineteenth century. Indeed, the shōguns who seized power after the heyday of the Minamotos were of lower rank and were themselves followed by men of rough military cast with none of the refinement associated with the Imperial Court.

Japanese culture, including the theatre, followed a similar pattern: the courtly culture of the Heian period seeped down into the lower nobility and thence into the warrior classes who, by the fourteenth century, had become the guardians of culture and had replaced the impoverished and totally powerless nobility. By the late seventeenth century, it was the merchants who, although placed at the bottom of the social hierarchy, actually held economic power and quickly became the center of the amazing cultural renaissance which marks the years at the turn of the seventeenth century. The destitute nobles and samurai were destined never to regain their place as custodians of culture, but they continued to influence it in three ways: through regulations, sumptuary laws and the like; through their image, a vestige of the past which was perpetuated in the popular theatre particularly; and through the arts they had developed and protected in the past, and which continued to condition and influence the development of popular arts sometimes directly and sometimes only obliquely.

Even while the major cultural achievements were in the hands of the nobility and the warrior class, however, popular arts were flourishing. Indeed, with the exception of the imported gagaku-bugaku, all the Japanese theatrical forms derive from popular entertainments, so that even when a "polished" form has become world-famous as an aristocratic art, as in the case of nō, it is based in the vigorous, often earthy, performances which belonged to the plebeians. Like a firm, steady ground bass beneath a baroque melody, the healthy, heady, popular element underlies and forms a kind of balance to the highly aesthetic elements which derived from the more refined or learned classes.

The legendary beginnings of Japanese theatre and dance (they are inseparable from the start) are firmly rooted in the earth, both literally and figuratively. According to the *Kojiki* (Record of Ancient Things, compiled in 712), the Sun Goddess, angered by pranks played by her mischievous brother, retired into a cavern and closed up the entrance with a stone, thereby casting the world into darkness. To lure her out the other gods gathered outside, and Heavenly-Alarming-Female, laying out a sounding board before the cave, began to perform an extravagant dance in which she pulled open the top of her costume and lifted her skirts—a kind of divine striptease. The gods were so pleased that they shook with laughter, piquing the curiosity of the Sun Goddess, who finally emerged from her cave.

Many of the elements found in this first performance were to prosper in later forms of Japanese entertainment: dance, eroticism, a sense of play, the foot striking the sounding board. This stamping sound is both a rhythmic device and a reminder of the physical presence of the performer and his connection with the earth. To this day, Heavenly-Alarming-Female's dance is commemorated, in very attenuated form, in the *kagura* or sacred dances at the Shinto shrines.

Aside from the imported bugaku, two dance forms of importance developed in Japan before the first major theatrical form, nō, was to prosper in the fourteenth century. They were *dengaku* and *sarugaku*, and both contributed enormously to the creation of nō; indeed, they were its immediate precursors, nō at first being called *sarugaku nō* (the skill of saragaku). Sarugaku was introduced from China in about the eighth century, but quickly

adapted to Japanese culture. At first it was made up of miscellaneous entertainments: songs, dances, acrobatics, juggling and
magic. Later, short comic plays were added, and little by little
the dramatic element became more important, until sarugaku
was more like a simple play with songs and dances interpolated
than like the variety program it had at first been. It was well
on its way to becoming the first highly developed theatrical
form in Japan.

Dengaku, the other popular form preceding nō, derives, as
its name "field music" suggests, from peasant songs and dances
which accompanied work in the rice fields. This folk dengaku
survives today, but it was soon taken over by professional performers and incorporated into other kinds of entertainment,
including sarugaku. It finally emerged as a kind of show combining song, dance and acrobatics, and became so popular in the
fourteenth century that writers claimed there was an epidemic
of dengaku fever. In fact, the fall of the Kamakura shogunate
in 1333 is often ascribed to the regent's passionate obsession
with dengaku.

With the fall of Kamakura off in the east, Kyoto once again
became the political as well as cultural capital of the country,
and the warriors in power there felt more strongly than ever
the refined influence of courtly tastes and manners. Politically,
under the Ashikaga shōguns, the country was in turmoil for
several centuries; but, far from being in a state of decadence,
the arts of Japan and her cultural life were fermenting and
beginning to blossom under the fertilizing impact of contact
and compromise between the two major elements of military
and civilian, or samurai and courtier.

There were other forces at work as well: during the Kamakura
period (1185–1333), Buddhism had become a popular religion
in Japan, no longer restricted to the noble classes. Finding a
relatively easy coexistence with Shinto, the native animistic
religion, Buddhism sometimes merged with it. A number of
great religious leaders arose and preached their gospels among
populace, warriors and nobles alike. Most important for their
impact on the theatre were two Buddhist sects: Jōdo, or Pure
Land, and Zen. The former was a distinctly popular form of
Buddhism calculated to appeal to the simple and downtrodden

during a time when they had little to look forward to in this life, and little assurance that they might not perish from one day to the next. Essentially, it taught that all men can receive the mercy of Buddha and be reborn in his Paradise if they will but repeat, with a pure believing heart, the name of Amida Buddha. Faith, not works, and the utterance of the magical name, even if only at the moment of death, offered a hope of eternal salvation. No wonder men of all walks, from beggars to emperors, became followers of the Jōdo sect, and practiced the repetition of the *nembutsu,* as it was called: *Namu Amida Butsu.* In all forms of traditional Japanese theatre, but most often in the nō plays, these words are heard time and again on the lips of characters about to die, or those who are expiating their attachment to human passions.

Curiously enough, however, it was the other form of Buddhism, Zen, which influenced the deeper meanings and the shape of the nō drama. The apparent simplicity, austerity, and vital experiential qualities of Zen appealed to the stern, unlearned warriors who were not inclined either to spend time in studying abstruse metaphysics or to accept the emotionalism inherent in other forms of Buddhism. Bypassing the written word, Zen attempts to go directly to the heart of the matter, hopefully arriving at enlightenment by a process of meditation, quiet introspection, and a leap beyond logic. So profoundly did the deep spirituality of Zen penetrate the Japanese arts and way of living during the Kamakura and Ashikaga shogunates that more than one historian has described Japan's finest arts as quintessentially Zen-inspired. However partial this view may be when seen in the perspective of Japan's rich cultural achievements, it is certainly applicable to a major portion of it, particularly to those arts which blossomed in the feudal period: nō, tea ceremony, calligraphy, ink painting, flower arrangement, rock gardens. The flamboyant side of the coin comes to the fore only at the end of the feudal period and is best represented in the flowering of popular arts in the seventeenth and eighteenth centuries.

The age that saw the zenith of sarugaku nō, now called simply nō, was the period of the samurai, but it was a warrior softened, or at any rate refined somewhat by his contact with the court.

Indeed, the shōguns for many decades were men of great elegance and refinement, living a life of learning and aesthetic pleasures in the exquisite Golden Pavilion which they had built on the outskirts of the capital. Newly rich, they gave themselves over to the meditative disciplines of the Zen arts, developed new forms of poetry, and once again turned their eyes toward the Chinese with whom they had reestablished relations.

The two most important steps in advancing sarugaku toward nō as we more or less know it today were taken shortly after the middle of the fourteenth century. In 1368, a well-known performer of sarugaku, Kannami, incorporated a special kind of dance known as *kuse mai* in his performance, thereby enriching both music and dance forms within sarugaku and making it more popular than ever. In 1374 Kannami and his eleven-year-old son, later to be known as Zeami, performed ceremonial sarugaku at the Imakumano shrine, where their performance was witnessed by the shōgun, Yoshimitsu. Apparently impressed by the skill of the nō, and struck by the childish beauty of Zeami, the sixteen-year-old shōgun took the troupe under his protection. From that day sarugaku nō quickly outstripped dengaku in both artistic achievement and popularity, and under the sensitive and brilliant leadership of Zeami, it reached a peak of perfection that remains unsurpassed in theatrical history.

Nō is a performing art integrating music, dance and speech in order to present, usually obliquely and often through reference to past events relived by a ghost, a simple situation or story. According to Zeami's treatises, which were written over a period of about thirty years and which covered all phases of the art from the most material to the most spiritual, nō reposes upon two foundations: *monomane*, or the imitation of things, which may be thought of as giving a certain realism to the performance, and *yūgen*, a difficult term whose basic meaning is mystery or depth, and which pulls nō in the direction of spirituality and unearthliness. For Zeami, a perfect balance is necessary, but nō has seldom managed that feat, and almost inevitably falls on the side of *yūgen*, attenuating the realistic elements so that they harmonize with the high stylization, refinement and elegance of the more spiritual elements.

Some viewers have refused to call nō theatre, comparing it rather to a ceremony. It is true that the spectator of nō must be closely in tune with the performers. Otherwise, he will miss entirely the experience which, somewhat akin to meditation, is led by the spiritual strength of the protagonist who, according to Zeami's prescriptions, must move only seven-tenths on the outside and ten-tenths on the inside. The slow pace requires patience, but the aesthetic rewards can be great. Nō is subtle, suggestive, and oblique, both in its text and its presentation. The reader who has not had the opportunity to witness a performance will find it difficult to imagine the exquisite refinement of the actor-dancer, the unearthly quality of the singing and chanting, and the dramatic impact of the sparse instrumental accompaniment of two or three drums and a flute punctuated by the sharp cries and guttural groans of the musicians.

The music, so strange to Western ears, underlies the entire rhythm and organization of a nō play, which falls into three parts: jo (introduction), ha (development) and kyū (finale). This structure, basic to most of the performing arts in Japan, derives from the old gagaku and bugaku of the Imperial court, and in nō regulates not only each play, but the series of five plays which, traditionally, were performed in a day-long program, with comic interludes (kyōgen) separating them. The two-hundred-odd nō plays in the repertoire today are divided into five groups, according to theme or major character *(shite)*, and each group represents a different aesthetic feeling which contributes to the total impact of the full program.

The first group is made up of god plays, works of an auspicious nature, celebrating perhaps a deity of some shrine. Their rhythm is slow and their action almost nonexistent. They are introductory pieces *(jo)* and must slowly prepare the spectator for the nō experience which is to follow. The next three groups belong to the development section *(ha)* of the program. Warrior plays, more complex and active than god plays, deal with the ghosts of dead warriors who are condemned to unrest because of their attachment to the world or for their sins while alive. For the *waki,* or secondary role, usually an itinerant priest, they re-enact a major event of their lives, often a battle, and ask the priest to pray for their repose. Women plays, perhaps the most refined of all the pieces, certainly containing the most concentrated dose of *yūgen,* make up the third group. The fourth group is miscellaneous, but contains a number of madwoman plays. They have none of the flamboyant romanticism which the Western reader associates with such themes. The madness is usually simply suggested by a branch carried by the major character. The final group *(kyū),* faster and more dramatic than the others, is made up of demon plays, no doubt the most accessible to the beginner, but frequently considered of lower rank by the nō connoisseur, who invariably prefers the understated elegance of the woman plays.

The deep spirituality of nō in its higher reaches is related to the spirit of Zen. Zeami himself was a practitioner of that philosophy, and one feels that the theatre he brought to full flower is, much like Zen, pointing beyond itself to an experience that transcends human expression. Zeami states it metaphorically: "At Shinra [an ancient Korean kingdom] at midnight, the sun is shining."

Actually there is more evident theatricality in the nō performance than one might at first think. Even in the more elegant works, the size, richness and striking colors and design of the costumes are essentially theatrical, as are many of the masks. And as a corrective to the otherworldliness or *yūgen* of nō, the plays in a typical day's performance are interspersed with the delightful kyōgen which, unlike nō, lean heavily in the direction of *monomane* or the imitation of things. These homely farces treat, in simple terms, many of the basic human relationships, showing men, and even gods, to be basically foolish, proud, vain, cowardly, avaricious, or devilishly clever when it comes to taking advantage of others.

Kyōgen (literally, "mad words"), derived from the comic elements in sarugaku and dengaku, are performed in a highly stylized way which accentuates their vitality and humor and suggests their relation to the nō, although never approaching the level of abstraction of nō. There is rarely music or dance; instead, dialogue dominates as the rogue outwits the fool in these delicious vignettes which have not lost their instant appeal.

After more than a century of protection by the Ashikagas,

nō once again became a popular form in the sixteenth century, and might well have developed into a theatre like kabuki. The Tokugawas, however, when they finally succeeded in centralizing political power, took over nō as their official ceremony, thus bringing about its coagulation into set forms and slowing down its pace which today, most critics agree, is about half what it was in Zeami's day. A text of a few pages, running for perhaps forty-five minutes in Zeami's day, now requires an hour and a half to perform.

While the Ashikaga shōguns were preoccupied with nō and other aesthetic, or at any rate nonpolitical, pursuits, the country was falling down around them. The centralized government established by the Minamotos in Kamakura gave way to a full-blown feudal state with warring barons fighting among themselves, and finally to a state of utter chaos which prevailed for most of the sixteenth century. This period is known in Japanese history as *sengoku,* the country at war. It was brought to an end by the ascension to power, one after another in rapid succession, of three of the greatest warriors and leaders in Japanese history: Oda Nobunaga, Toyotomi Hideyoshi, and Tokugawa Ieyasu.

The accomplishment of Nobunaga was to destroy the strength of many powerful houses and to take possession of all the central provinces of Japan, including, of course, Kyoto, the capital. When Hideyoshi followed him in 1584, he subjugated the rest of the outlying feudal estates and, by 1590, brought peace to the country for the first time in over a hundred years. Upon Hideyoshi's death in 1598, Ieyasu's power was contested by several powerful families, including adherents to the son of Hideyoshi. In 1600, however, Ieyasu won a definitive victory at the battle of Sekigahara, and in 1603 was named shōgun by the emperor. In 1615 he destroyed the remains of Hideyoshi's family adherents, and from that time until 1868 the Tokugawas occupied the shōgun's seat, although, as had been customary in the past, the real power was often wielded by a regent.

From the Kamakura period to the reign of the Tokugawas, Japan had witnessed the growth and firm establishment of the warrior class as the ruling power and as guardian of culture.

It had seen also the development of the so-called "Way of the Warrior," *bushidō*, which, ideally at any rate, elevated loyalty and courage to the highest virtues and set up a code of behavior—austere, manly, and impassively stern—which influenced almost every facet of Japanese life until the nineteenth century, and is strongly reflected in the kabuki and bunraku (puppet) theatres. With the coming of peace under the Tokugawas, the warrior was denied the very activity which seemed his *raison d'être,* and he posed a grave problem to public tranquility. Curiously enough, it was only in the eighteenth century, centuries after it had lost its vitality, that the word *bushidō* came to be used, and the practices of the "Way of the Warrior" codified.

The two hundred fifty years of the Tokugawa period marked the rise of the townsmen and merchants to a role of economic and artistic importance in Japan. Where the warriors had formerly been arbiters of taste, now the merchant class took over that role. The shōguns, in an effort to stabilize their power and save it from the deleterious effects of change, promulgated edicts which discouraged social flexibility. At the top of the social scale were the samurai, and just below them the peasants who supplied the country with its chief means of subsistence, rice. Third were the artisans, and at the bottom the merchants *(chōnin).* The social mobility, which had existed briefly during the Ashikaga rule and had actually allowed the rise of a humble foot soldier like Hideyoshi to the role of virtual ruler of Japan, was once more impeded by Hideyoshi himself and his successors. In 1585, ordinances were issued forbidding men of whatsoever station to leave their employ without special permission.

Ironically enough, it was the lowly merchant class that was to furnish the economic force of the Tokugawa years; by as early as 1700 all the gold and silver in the country was in the hands of the merchant class, to whom the military and even the nobles were sorely in debt. The traditional rice economy, which the shogunate insisted lay at the base of its wealth, was only a relic of the past, and the true strength lay in the hands of the *chōnin.* This economic lie is at the foundation of many of the Tokugawas' economic problems, for here as elsewhere their inherent conservatism denied what was already fact and kept Japan in the Middle Ages far past the period of her natural development.

Indicative of this conservatism was the official attitude toward incursions from the West. At first friendly and even encouraging to Dutch and Portuguese merchants and to Christian missionaries, the rulers soon grew suspicious of their real intentions, and missionaries and converts alike were cruelly persecuted. After 1640 ports were closed to all foreign ships with the exception of a few Dutch ships a year. Likewise, no travel was permitted Japanese outside the country, and for more than two hundred years there was only minimal contact with developments in the rest of the world.

Within the country, at peace for the first time in centuries—although under the heel of a conservative military dictatorship—a new cultural renaissance was in the making. Indeed, indications of its character were evident as early as 1576 when Nobunaga built his luxurious Azuchi castle, famed for its brilliant decorations and bright coloring, set off with lavish use of gold leaf. The antipode of the austere Zen style preferred a century earlier, it announces the joyous hedonism and spirited sensuality which were to reign during the popular renaissance of the late seventeenth century. The culture of the merchants offers a happy contrast to the "Way of the Warrior." Although the *chōnin* often tried to emulate the samurai, even in the ethical standards he imposed upon himself (at least in the idealized picture which emerges from the popular theatre), he essentially represents a more carefree and liberated outlook, and offers a healthy balance to the stern ethics of *bushidō*.

There is a tendency among foreigners to think of Japanese arts in terms of the austere Zen-inspired forms which in Japan are sometimes characterized as *shibui* or astringent. Typical as well are the joyous color and spirited movement of Imari pottery, of Momoyama architecture, and of the kabuki theatre. In Japanese arts taken as a whole, there is an immense range and an impressive balance, with the *shibui* at the one extreme and the flamboyantly colorful, the *hade*, at the other.

Just as gagaku-bugaku reflects the courtly orientation of Japanese culture in the Heian period, and nō the refined warrior aesthetics of the Ashikaga shōguns, kabuki reflects the popular culture that begins to dominate with the Tokugawa rule. Kabuki was created by and for the townsmen, and depended upon their approval and enthusiasm for its very existence. Late in the sixteenth century, or perhaps early in the seventeenth, there appeared among the popular entertainers who customarily offered their performances in the dry river bed of the Kamo River in Kyoto, Okuni, a woman who was attached to the ancient shrine at Izumo. Her dancing of the *nembutsu*—a prayer dance of Buddhist origin, but now debased and blended with comic and folk elements—found the favor of a large public, and soon others joined with her or emulated her. Before long, groups performing similar dances developed, and because they were made up of rather unsavory characters—prostitutes, pimps, hangers-on—people not quite acceptable in decent society, they were known as *kabuki-mono,* kabuki things or people. Kabuki was derived from a now obsolete verb, *kabuku,* "to be aslant." In 1629 the shogunate forbade the performances of women's kabuki claiming it was corrupting the samurai. Young men stepped into the breach and performed all the roles, bringing along with them some of the acrobatic elements of the dengaku they had previously performed. In 1652 they were outlawed for reasons similar to those given in banning women's kabuki. With this step, kabuki's artistic development could begin in earnest, performed by *yarō* or mature men. Quickly the simple scenes and erotic dances of the first half of the century developed into a more sophisticated theatrical form: lengthy plays with incredibly complicated plots, a variety of characters, and families of actors specializing in particular types of roles.

In western Japan where the courtly influence of Kyoto was still felt, the commoners wished to emulate the refinement of the aristocrats and, at the same time, to see themselves represented on the stage. For them, a special style of elegant and refined acting developed, and plays were written dealing with the problems of the merchant class. Called *sewamono,* or domestic problem plays, they reflect in idealized form the lives of the city dwellers, and give an important role to the women in the pleasure districts which had come into prominence about this time. Ill-fated loves between *chōnin* and geisha were depicted with endless variations, often ending in stylized travel scenes in dance form which led to double love suicides. Such a romantic aura came to surround the love suicides depicted in the plays that the impressionable spectators too often found it the logical way out of their own personal dilemmas, and the government placed a ban on the theme.

Many plays of this kind were written by Chikamatsu Monzaemon, universally recognized as the greatest dramatic genius of Japan. Writing for the great actor of refined young lover roles, Sakata Tōjūrō, Chikamatsu brought the kabuki to its literary zenith in the Osaka–Kyoto region toward the end of the seventeenth century. But Chikamatsu wrote plays of different kinds, and soon turned to writing for the puppets who were at this time beginning to compete for popularity with the kabuki actors.

At the same time, in eastern Japan, an actor of genius, Ichikawa Danjūrō, was developing his own style to conform to the tastes of the merchants and the toughs from eastern Japan who had settled in the brash frontier town of Edo, as Tokyo was then called. The military capital of the country, it was filled with swaggering samurai—proud men who alone were permitted to wear two swords, and had the legal right to cut down any commoner who showed them disrespect. Danjūrō realized his audience would enjoy living the lives of the samurai, transposed to a theatrical key and made bigger than life. He developed a style known as *aragoto,* rough style, in which movement, wigs, costumes, everything, conspired to give the impression of gigantic size and strength. Black and red lines, sometimes blue, violet and other colors as well, stressed the musculature of the face and limbs. Great stamping feet and energetic arrangements of the limbs, culminating in the crossing of one eye, resulted in the climactic poses known as *mie* which have become a standard technique of any heroic kabuki presentation.

The color, vigor and sensuality of *aragoto* and of the tragedies of love in the gay quarters suggest the spirit of the period that is known as Genroku. Strictly speaking, it is the years from 1688 to 1703, but as a state of mind and spirit it embraces several decades beyond those dates and represents the first full expression of popular culture—the flamboyant attitudes to art and life that are apparent from the beginning of the Tokugawa period and even before. The commoners, sensitive to the more aristocratic arts of earlier years, were able to free themselves from their influence and give birth to arts that were purely Japanese and imbued with their love of life, vitality, luxury and sensuous appeal.

Intimately related to the arts, and above all to the kabuki, were the so-called gay quarters where women of all ranks, from the common street walkers to the grandiose courtisans who received a king's ransom for one night, were available to the young man in search of pleasure. Here the arts of music, song and dance grew as accomplishments requisite in the entertaining of the refined townsmen, and here the woodblock prints which so spiritedly depict this world were developed. Known as *ukiyo-e,* or pictures of the floating world, they reveal the glamorous side of that fickle world of life which passes like a dream. And next to this prospered the dramatic actor-prints which were collected by the fans of the men who were the matinee idols of their day, and who exercised an immense influence on contemporary speech, clothing and behavior.

As kabuki matured, the movements, costumes, poses, and speech patterns of the great actors came to be regarded as definitive, and the highly choreographed character of the performance became more pronounced. In the early periods, the *onnagata,* or men who specialized in women's roles, were the only ones to perform dances but in the eighteenth century, *tachiyaku,* or actors of male roles, began to perform dances as well, and the kabuki dance was born.

The dance play came to form an important part of the kabuki repertoire, along with the *sewamono* and the heroic and highly stylized history play *(jidaimono)* based on Japan's past and her legends. A standard kabuki program today usually includes one play of each type, although during other periods the differing types of plays were sometimes written into a single monstrous play lasting ten hours or more.

Since kabuki had apparently outgrown its immoral beginnings, it was decided to write its name in a different manner. Three Chinese characters were chosen, but were pronounced in their pseudo-Chinese manner: KA (the native Japanese is *uta* for the same character), meaning song, formed the first syllable; BU (*mai* in its Japanese reading), dance, was the second; and KI, or performance, the third. Thus the new way of writing kabuki was almost a definition of its theatrical form: a performance containing song and dance. Unlike Western musicals, however, kabuki totally integrates all elements of the production so that the actor is at one and the same time an actor-dancer-singer.

Kabuki could not have developed into its present complex total theatre form without the contribution of a number of other theatrical forms, most notably the puppet or doll theatre, often called bunraku, after the name of the man who revived the dying art in the early nineteenth century. The puppet theatre arose about the same time as kabuki, and reached the first high point in its history when Chikamatsu, growing tired of the liberties the actor-centered kabuki took with his plays, decided to devote himself to the puppet theatre. He combined his talents with those of a singer-narrator of great genius, Gidayū, whose name is now used to designate the singing style which accompanies the puppet play.

The bunraku is a composite theatrical art made up of three important elements: the puppets and their manipulators, the narrator, and the *shamisen* accompaniment. Each of these arts had begun independently of the others and finally they merged toward the end of the seventeenth century into the most serious and literate puppet theatre in the world. Reciters, as early as the fifteenth century, had accompanied themselves on the *biwa*, a kind of lute, as they sang the story of a certain Princess Jōruri. This tale was to become the prototype of the narrative element in bunraku, and the name *jōruri* is now applied to the narrative singing style, and is oftentimes used synonymously with bunraku.

The shamisen, a three-stringed banjo-like instrument, forms the chief accompaniment for both puppet and kabuki. It came from China via the Ryukyu Islands about the middle of the sixteenth century, and soon replaced the biwa as the accompaniment for the jōruri. After the middle of the seventeenth century the jōruri and its shamisen were used to accompany puppet performances. Slowly the puppets were improved, and at the same time the literary elements developed. Chikamatsu wrote history plays showing off the fantastic possibilities of the puppets, and in 1703 wrote his first *sewamono*, the famous domestic tragedy, *The Love Suicides at Sonezaki.*

It was after Chikamatsu's death in 1734 that the large puppets manipulated by three visible puppeteers were first used. It is these puppets, with their highly expressive heads and the complex manipulations permitted by three operators working in close harmony, which are identified with bunraku today. The puppet theatre enjoyed its zenith of popularity during the 1730s, 40s and 50s. Some of the perennial masterpieces of the repertoire were written during this period by a group of playwrights headed by Takeda Izumo I: *Sugawara's Secrets of Calligraphy* (in no. **13**, freely translated by Ernst as *The House of Sugawara)*, *Yoshitsune and the Thousand Cherry Trees* (untranslated), and *Chūshingura* (no. **3**). Although by the mid-eighteenth century the puppet theatre had fallen on lean days from which it never fully recovered (even though writers of talent continued to enrich its repertoire, notably Chikamatsu Hanji), so great was the puppet theatre's popularity at this time that it overshadowed the kabuki.

In order to regain their lead, the kabuki actors began to borrow not only the plays, but the very techniques of the puppet theatre. This enriched their performances immensely and introduced the new world of jōruri music into the theatre of living actors. At times the imitation of puppets is so extreme that an actor moves with expressionless face and unarticulated hands while he is "operated" by several visible black-clad "puppeteers". For many years there was a fruitful borrowing back and forth between the two theatres. Today the kabuki repertoire is made up largely of classics which were originally written for the puppets. The above-mentioned plays by Izumo I are, in fact, listed as the three masterpieces in the *jidaimono* category of the kabuki repertoire.

The eighteenth century was a great period of growth for the kabuki. It saw the development of theatre music into an abundant and varied accompaniment which was closely integrated with the movements and speech of the actor-dancers. Drawing on nō and popular and folk elements, theatre music attained an unprecedented richness and expressiveness. The eighteenth century also saw the rise of the dance choreographers, as opposed to the actors who had originally invented their own dances. This led to the luxuriant period of dances in the early nineteenth century, from which many dances survive to this day as classics of the repertoire. The eighteenth century was also a period of important developments in the physical theatre. Notably the revolving stage was added—used commonly in the kabuki more than a hundred years before its adoption in the · West, if it can be said to have been really adopted in the West. Elevators appeared on the stage, and most important of all, the *hanamichi* was extended as a kind of bridge-stage connecting the stage proper with the back of the auditorium. This permitted the actors to make their entrances and exits through the audience, posing at a focal point. This development stressed the intimacy between the actors and the audience which is an important factor in the aesthetics of kabuki.

In the early nineteenth century kabuki was again in its heyday, and, catering to the tastes of its public as always, it created works that delighted the audiences of a period known for its decadence. As the strength of the Tokugawa shogunate declined, and that of the military caste as well, the true power of the merchant class became more and more apparent until finally the military and merchant classes were to merge in the latter part of the nineteenth century. In the meantime, playwrights like Tsuruya Namboku IV were writing works which allowed for the use of dazzling stage tricks while depicting the seamy side of life as men saw it around them. Rather than glamorizing the masterless samurai, or *rōnin*, who had proliferated by this time and had become a real social problem, he revealed the chaotic state of a society which was ready for upheaval. With Namboku a new kind of realism enters into kabuki and is taken up by the greatest kabuki writer of the nineteenth century, Kawatake Mokuami, whose plays remain widely performed today. He is the master of *kizewamono* or raw domestic plays, centering usually on the adventures of criminals, prostitutes and the like. *Benten the Thief* (in no. **13**) and *The Love of Izayoi and Seishin* (no. **62**) are two of his best-known works and typical of the genre.

Spanning the last years of the Tokugawa rule and the first years of the Meiji Restoration (1868) when power was once again returned to the Imperial house, Mokuami is a link between the old kabuki and the new plays which today continue to be written in emulation of Western forms of theatre. When the Japanese once again opened their ports to foreign vessels and cast their eyes abroad, they were as eager to import the Western culture they found in Victorian Europe as they had been to import Chinese culture centuries earlier. The traditional theatre arts were in a real danger of perishing; in their enthusiasm for all things Western, even the kabuki actors sometimes tended to throw over the old classic styles and bring into kabuki a kind of realism that was incompatible with the high theatricality and the integration of music, dance and performance which have always been essential elements of kabuki.

The little creative vitality shown by kabuki in the twentieth century is found chiefly in dance pieces. When the shogunate collapsed, nō theatre, long protected by the shōguns, almost vanished with it. It was saved largely due to the efforts of a minor actor, Umewaka Minoru, who continued to perform in a theatre in Tokyo. Now that nō no longer belonged exclusively to the samurai, the kabuki actors could more easily pillage that repertoire; dating from the end of the nineteenth century are some of the more famous kabuki versions of nō plays such as *Funa Benkei* (Benkei in the Boat) and *The Maple Viewing (Momiji Gari)*, and some of the delightful kabuki versions of kyōgen, all of which are performed as dance plays. Aside from these adaptations, the new plays written for kabuki, with very rare exceptions, have been disappointing; the texts make little use of techniques long identified with kabuki, and take this gigantic form away from the integrated total kind of theatre which it had become. The new kabuki is heading in the direction of Western theatre in a more realistic mode, depending almost entirely on dialogue: the antithesis of kabuki at its zenith. The greatest name among writers of neo-kabuki is Okamoto Kidō.

The great kabuki classics continue to be performed, but because they are now museum pieces, there is little creative imagination deployed in their performance in spite of the magnificent art exhibited by the actors, musicians and stage workers of this highly disciplined world. Hopefully playwrights and actors of genius and imagination will create, in the future, works that combine both the high style and total arts of kabuki and the rapid rhythms and meaningful content which seem essential to a popular theatre today.

As Westernization made greater inroads, the Japanese theatre in the late nineteenth century created new dramatic forms, notably *shimpa*, a hybrid of kabuki and Western melodrama, often described by Western writers as a sort of soap opera. Its appeal today is limited and it will probably disappear, mourned by few, within the next few generations. The other Western form is *shingeki*, "new theatre," and embraces all the plays written, whether by foreigners or by Japanese, in the modes deriving from the West. Probably nowhere are playwrights like Chekhov, Giraudoux and Brecht as popular as they are in Japan. The works of these playwrights and their offspring, covering an immense range of styles, ideologies, and qualities, are imitated by Japanese playwrights. The most famous of the playwrights is Mishima Yukio, who, although best known in the West for his novels, wrote dozens of plays including some of the most successful modern kabuki plays, adaptations of nō, and plays completely in the style of modern Western drama. The novelist Abe Kōbō has also ventured into theatre with the experimental *Friends*. But shingeki, most critics agree, has not yet come of age. Many observe that the future of Japanese theatre lies not in imitation of Western models, but in an integration of these new modes with Japan's traditional forms. If we look at the best of Japan's ancient arts, this seems a valid conclusion, for many of her most typical art forms were originally introduced from abroad, but through the years were adjusted to the spirit and mentality of the Japanese, and took on a shape which is universally recognized today as essentially and typically Japanese. There are signs of this happening already in the theatre, reflected not only in the works of Mishima, but in the highly experimental efforts of playwright-directors like Kara Jūrō who blends modern and ancient, East and West, Beckett, Artaud, Sophocles, and kabuki into a frenzied pop art product performed in his famous red tent. His plays are published and his theatrical ventures chronicled in the only English-language magazine devoted exclusively to Japanese theatre, *Concerned Theatre Japan* (see Further Readings). This recently founded periodical is devoted overwhelmingly to the most modern developments in Japanese theatre, but it occasionally relates contemporary to traditional forms, and reflects the theatrical ferment in Japan today.

The student consulting this bibliography will perhaps be struck by the small number of works available in English. In a sense, this is not surprising, since up until World War II, Japan remained a relatively exotic area of study. Because theatre, among all the arts, requires an almost immediate understanding (at least on a simple level), it demands more familiarity than forms like painting and poetry. Moreover, Japanese theatre, unlike the theatre we know best in the West, communicates at least as much through its performance techniques as it does through its text. Consequently a true appreciation of it depends to some extent upon the possibility of experiencing the play in the theatre. In recent years this has become more of a possibility, thanks to tours abroad, although infrequent, of kabuki, nō and kyōgen troupes, as well as more remote groups like the gagaku and various folk ensembles. In addition, films of the major dramatic forms are available through the Japanese Consulates throughout this country, and on loan from the Japan Society in New York. The importance of such aids in appreciating Japanese theatre cannot be too strongly stressed. Anyone wishing to undertake a production of one of these plays should, of course, turn to these films for a better grasp of the styles involved. Next best to the films are the magnificent photographs found in books like the Kōdansha publications (nos. **23, 47, 50**).

For the reader's convenience, the following divisions have been made in the bibliographical items. The first section is made up of studies which are comprehensive in nature, dealing either with Asian theatre, including Japanese, or with various phases of Japanese theatre. Among them are volumes which should be consulted for specific genres, and these are cross-referenced at the beginning of the appropriate genre section.

Three general works might be pointed out as of particular interest to the student making his first contact with the subject: items 1, 2, and 10.

The anthologies listed under this comprehensive heading include plays from countries other than Japan, or works of more than one genre. A particularly rewarding volume, both for the texts and for the finely chiseled introductions, is item 13.

The second section is devoted to nō and kyōgen, since they both belong to the same tradition and are usually treated in the same books. For introductory studies of the nō, one could do no better than turn to items 19, 21, 23 and 28 (the second item is somewhat more specialized than the others). For nō texts, 30 and 35 offer excellent examples and comments, and for kyōgen, 31 and 34 are de rigueur.

Kabuki and the puppet theatre have exercised such influence on each other that it is necessary to treat them in the same section. If the number of entries is any indication, they are indeed the popular theatres of Japan, with foreign scholars as well as in their own traditional development. Items 39, 40, and particularly 41 and 50 offer excellent introductions to kabuki, and item 47 is most highly recommended for the bunraku. Outstanding kabuki or puppet texts are found in items 60, 63, 13 and 15.

The next section treats all remaining facets of traditional theatre in Japan, including music and dance, and the final section is devoted to modern drama. There are usually only a few items for each category in these last two sections since much more attention has been given to the major traditional forms than to the more esoteric or contemporary forms. This is as it should be, for the traditional theatres are the foundation on which the student must build his understanding of what is peculiarly Japanese.

There are, the reader will note, a number of good general studies of each of the traditional theatres. Scholarly works have reached the point where they must now go on to more specialized topics of literary or dramatic interest, looking at stylistic peculiarities of the nō theatre, for example, or the religious elements in nō, the particular and universal comedy of kyōgen, makeup of kabuki, structure of puppet and kabuki drama, and such. A few specialized works exist, like P. G. O'Neill's study of nō's beginnings, and Charles Dunn's monograph on the early puppet theatre, or Ruth Shaver's book on kabuki costumes, and William P. Malm's outstanding works on Japanese music.

With play texts we are in a much less favorable position, but this is due to several factors. First of all, the texts offer many difficulties because of age and poetic techniques. Secondly, the text is only part of the theatrical production, much less important than in Western theatre, and the translator perhaps questions the possibility of suggesting the theatrical experience through the text alone. For this reason, the most recent texts of kabuki, like those of Brandon, or those of A. C. Scott even some years ago, give detailed descriptions of the stage movement, a distinct aid to the reader, but perhaps not fully appreciated by those unfamiliar with the plays in performance. As films become more available and theatre tours more frequent, it is to be hoped that more translations will appear.

Forty or fifty nō plays exist in acceptable translations or better. The kabuki and puppet plays available in English, however, are limited to about thirty, many of them in partial versions or without adequate stage directions. Thirteen plays by Chikamatsu, three by Mokuami, only two of the three favorite history plays, and very little from the period 1750 to 1830, one of the richest periods of kabuki history, are to be found in translation. One would like to see adequate versions of such favorites as *Yoshitsune Sembonzakura* (Yoshitsune and the Thousand Cherry Trees), *Natsumatsuri Naniwa Kagami* (Summer Festival in Osaka), or some of the master works of Chikamatsu Hanji, like *Honchō Nijūshiko* (Twenty-four Expressions of Filial Piety) and *Imoseyama Onna Teikin* (An Example of Noble Womanhood), not to mention such well-known pieces as *Tōkaidō Yotsuya Kaidan* (Yotsuya Ghost Story) and *Sannin Kichiza* (Three Men called Kichiza), or any number of famous adaptations from nō and kyōgen made toward the end of the nineteenth century.

As a matter of fact, a number of the above plays, and others not mentioned, are at this moment being translated or edited for publication, so the reader should be on the lookout for them. When we consider that an overwhelmingly large percentage of the play-texts annotated here were translated within the past seventeen years, we may indeed be optimistic. The next decade should offer a multiplicity of valuable new translations and substantial specialized studies as we become better acquainted with the theatrical treasures which lie in wait across the Pacific. They offer exciting possibilities in themselves and point out new directions that our theatre in the West might explore and pursue.

Brief Chronology of Japanese History and Theatre

A.D. 400	Recorded history begins in Japan.
560–571	Buddhism introduced into Japan.
701	Gagaku-ryō, the Imperial Music Department, founded.
710–782	Nara the capital. Period of Chinese influence.
782–1185	Heian period.
794	Capital founded in Heian-kyō (today's Kyoto).
11th century	Dengaku and sarugaku popular.
1156–1185	Rise and fall of the Taira family regents.
1185	Defeat of Taira (Heike) by Minamoto (Genji).
1185–1333	Kamakura period.
1333–1573	Ashikaga period.
1349	Famous dengaku performance in Kyoto in which the stalls collapsed.
1368	Kannami uses kuse mai in sarugaku nō.
1374	Yoshimitsu sees Kannami and Zeami perform and begins to protect sarugaku nō.
1400–1436	Zeami writes his essays on nō aesthetics
16th century	Sengoku: the country at war.
late 16th century	Nobunaga and Hideyoshi unify the country.
1573–1600	Momoyama period. Flowering of colorful arts.
1590	Edo (Tokyo) founded.
1593–1596	Hideyoshi performs in nō.
1600	Ieyasu's definitive victory at Sekigahara.
1603–1868	Tokugawa period. Nō becomes official ceremonial.
1603	Ieyasu named shōgun, celebrates with nō performance. Okuni performs her dances in Kyoto.
1615	Puppet jōruri presented in Edo.
1617–1641	Persecution of Christians. Expulsion of Spaniards, then Portuguese. All Europeans excluded. Dutch confined to Dejima in Nagasaki.

1629	Woman's kabuki forbidden.
1652	Young men's kabuki forbidden, theatres closed.
1653	Mature men's kabuki begins.
1664	First full-length kabuki plays produced.
1673	Danjūrō introduces aragoto style.
1678	Sakata Tōjūrō flourishes in Kyoto–Osaka.
1685	Gidayū opens his puppet theatre in Osaka with Chikamatsu as writer.
1688–1703	Genroku. Flowering of popular culture.
1703	Chikamatsu's *Love Suicides at Sonezaki*, first double suicide play. Chikamatsu flourished until 1724.
1746–1748	Composition of three puppet history plays destined to become major history plays in kabuki as well: *Sugawara's Secrets of Calligraphy, Yoshitsune and the Thousand Cherry Trees,* and *Chūshingura.*
1753	First use of large stage elevator in kabuki.
1758	First use of revolving stage in kabuki.
1766–1780	Chikamatsu Hanji flourishes.
1825	*Yotsuya Ghost Story,* most famous kabuki ghost play, representative of decadent late Tokugawa tastes and society.
1840	*Kanjinchō*, major kabuki work based on nō.
1854	Treaties between Japan and United States.
1854–1890	Kawatake Mokuami, major nineteenth-century kabuki writer, flourishes.
1868–1912	Meiji Restoration. Shōgun resigns, emperor becomes political head, capital moved to Tokyo. Nō troupes disband.
1878–1881	New nō stages built in Tokyo.
1887	Emperor first witnesses kabuki performance.
1911	Major neo-kabuki play, Okamoto Kidō's *Shūzenji Monogatari* (The Mask Maker).
1928	First kabuki tour abroad: Russia.
1955	Kabuki tour to People's Republic of China.
1960	First kabuki tour to the United States. Since

this date almost each year has seen a tour of
some traditional Japanese theatre either to the
United States or to Europe.
1966   National Theatre opens.

ANNOTATED
BIBLIOGRAPHY

General Works: Criticism

1. Lombard, Frank Alanson. *An Outline History of the Japanese Drama*. London: George Allen and Unwin, 1928; Boston: Houghton, Mifflin Co., 1929. 358 pp.

A resident of many years in Japan, and longtime professor of English at two universities in Kyoto, Professor Lombard was able to bring a firsthand knowledge of Japanese theatricals to his research at a time when most books on Japanese theatre were written from a distance, or without an intimate contact. This is the first effort in English to present a comprehensive picture of Japanese theatre, and most of what the *Outline History* contains still stands. More than an outline, this work is in fact an anthology, embracing all the traditional forms of Japanese drama. The explanatory material is slight when compared to the number of pages devoted to translations.

The author gives careful attention to the earliest forms of dance, song, and quasi-theatre in Japan, a field often lightly glossed over. Shrine dances and street fairs are described, as well as the more recognized antecedents of nō: *dengaku* and *sarugaku*. Of these latter, several interesting translations are given, along with sensitive renderings of seven nō plays. Lombard does not overlook the kyōgen, the comic interludes in the nō performance, which are described and represented by a translation of *Busu*. The *Mibu kyōgen*, attached to Buddhist services, are also discussed in some detail.

A short introduction to the puppet theatre precedes a lengthy translation of *The Soga Revenge*, a *jōruri* written by Chikamatsu Monzaemon for the puppets in 1718. A lively and moving version which conveys some of the archaic feeling of the jōruri language, this is, aside from Keene's *Battles of Coxinga* (in no. 60), the only history play by the master of Japanese drama available in English. As such, it is a precious example of that heroic and histrionic form.

A brief description of kabuki's history is followed by a translation of *The Death-Love of Kamiya-Jihei*, an early nineteenth-century kabuki version of a play that is a corruption of Chikama-tsu's masterpiece, *The Love Suicides at Amijima* of 1721 (in nos. **57, 60**).

This is a richly rewarding book either for the beginner or for the more knowledgeable student in search of interesting and well-translated texts. For the latter, of course, the texts will be more meaningful, for there are few illustrations and little material to help one imagine the style of the performance for the various kinds of plays.

2. Bowers, Faubion. *Japanese Theatre*. New York: Hermitage House, 1952. xxi, 294 pp. (Paperback, Hill and Wang, Dramabook).

This was the first book dealing with Japanese theatre to be written after World War II, and remains one of the most lively, colorful, and interesting studies of a varied and complex subject. The author tells us in his preface that he will treat the theatre arts as they exist in Japan today (1952) together with their history. Since kabuki was for many centuries the dominant theatrical form in Japan, it is natural that it occupy most of the space in the book.

In a clearly organized first chapter, Bowers treats the legendary origins of Japanese dance and the beginnings of Japanese theatre. His treatment of this very complicated subject is typical of the entire book; it is explicit, sophisticated, vivid, witty, clear and informative, with attention given not only to the bare essentials, but also to interpretation and the underlying aesthetics. The author is particularly strong in drawing generalizations from a wealth of material.

After a description of the early developments in kabuki, the book turns in some detail to one of the greatest periods of kabuki's history, the Genroku (roughly 1688–1720). With plentiful examples, the author distinguishes between the kinds of theatre that developed in western and in eastern Japan, giving many summaries of plays, and occasionally a brief translated excerpt. Many of these plays are not yet available in complete English translation.

In other chapters, Bowers admirably treats the various aspects of kabuki and summarizes its aesthetic conventions. The more politically involved theatre of the twentieth century and the inroads made by realism are discussed in two final chapters.

A valuable appendix offers translations of three kabuki plays of varying types: *Tsuchigumo* (The Monstrous Spider) is a nineteenth-century dance play based on a nō drama; *Sesshū Gappō ga Tsuji* (Gappo and his Daughter Tsuji) is the one famous act from a lengthy eighteenth-century puppet play; *Sukeroku* is one of the most famous and beloved of the flamboyant plays belonging to the Ichikawa family and dates from the early eighteenth century. While certain passages are shortened or deleted altogether, these versions remain, as of 1972, the only translations available of these popular plays.

Written over twenty years ago, this work does not, of course, reflect recent advances in Japanese theatre scholarship, and occasionally factual details may be slightly askew. However, its warmth, enthusiasm, personal tone, and breadth of scope make it one of the most spirited introductions to Japanese theatre.

3. Haar, Francis, photographer. *Japanese Theatre in Highlight: A Pictorial Commentary.* 2d ed. Text by Earle Ernst. Rutland, Vermont and Tokyo: Charles E. Tuttle Co., 1954. 127 pp.

This slim volume of black-and-white photographs offers an introduction to the world of Japanese theatre, with its important visual aspects. The photos are clear and varied, covering the three major theatre forms—nō, bunraku (puppet), and kabuki —both onstage and backstage. Each of the three sections is preceded by a page-and-a-half introduction, and the photos themselves are accompanied by explanations that touch on theatre structures, staging, acting techniques, musical accompaniments, masks, costumes, puppets, and so forth. While the book is brief and necessarily succinct, the captions give focus to the photos, thus aiding the viewer to see significant points.

4. Keene, Donald. *Japanese Literature: An Introduction for West-*

ern Readers. Paperbound. New York: Grove Press, Evergreen Books, 1955. 114 pp.

This tiny volume, with its unpretentious title, offers more than many volumes twice its size. For the reader eager to understand the literary details of Japanese theatre, the introduction will explain how stylistic peculiarities fit into the general history of Japanese literature, and how the language itself has fostered some of these. Suggestive detail, digressiveness, a lack of structural tightness, and the use of imitation in a virtuoso approach to creativity are all discussed. The chapter devoted to theatre deals only with nō and the doll theatre, since kabuki texts rarely exhibit the literary values of the two other forms. The history of each is briefly traced, along with its particularities as a performing art. Appropriate analogies are made to Western forms of theatre. The texts of nō are given some attention, while in the discussion of the puppet theatre the question of stylization and realism is taken up.

Although the final chapter, "Japanese Literature under Western Influence," scarcely touches on theatre, it is full of insights into the differences between Japanese and Western ways of approaching literature, insights which the imaginative reader might well carry over into his considerations concerning theatre.

5. Bowers, Faubion. *Theatre in the East: A Survey of Asian Dance and Drama.* New York: Thomas Nelson and Sons, 1956. 374 pp. (Paperback, Grove Press, Evergreen Books).

By the author's admission, a work like *Theatre in the East* is "essentially a journalistic report of what dance and drama in Asia is like today." It is necessarily incomplete, since the area and periods it covers are so vast. Beginning with India, then plunging southward to Ceylon, the author moves slowly up the southeast coast of Asia through Burma, Thailand, Cambodia and Laos; then he follows the archipelago into Malaya, Indonesia and the Philippines. Finally he travels up the east coast of Asia through China, Vietnam and Hong Kong, stopping briefly in Okinawa before arriving at his final destination, Japan.

Bowers discusses separately the drama and the dance for each country where this is appropriate, and there is a special section on drama today for countries where this has significance.

The forty pages devoted to Japan begin with a few general observations: they compare the situation in Japan with that of other Asian countries, and stress the richness and variety of theatres and dance available in Japan. Taking the theatrical forms in chronological order, Bowers discusses first the ancient court music and dance, *gagaku* and *bugaku,* and the aristocratic nō. To kabuki he gives the most space, describing personal experiences and treating new developments in the kabuki world. The puppets are treated briefly, and a few generalizations are made about the role of dance in Japanese theatre. A final section deals with the modern Japanese theatre, which is Western oriented.

Theatre in the East is easy to read, written in a lively style, illustrated by personal reminiscences, and full of valuable generalizations. The breadth of scope makes for a certain thinness and leads occasionally to errors in factual detail, although the spirit is always conveyed with fidelity and vigor. While this book is most valuable for its overview of Asian theatre, the beginner would do well to go on to more detailed studies like Bowers's own *Japanese Theatre* (no. **2**).

6. Komiya Toyotaka, ed. *Japanese Music and Drama in the Meiji Era.* Tr. by Edward G. Seidensticker and Donald Keene. Japanese Culture in the Meiji Era, vol. 3. Tokyo: Ōbunsha, 1956. xiii, 535 pp.

The Meiji Era (1868–1912) brought great changes in the cultural life of Japan, for after a period of some two hundred fifty years, the country was at last opened to outside influences. In their eagerness to embrace Western ways, the Japanese overlooked their own rich traditions. For the theatre arts, then, it was a complex period of revolutionary and counterrevolutionary currents and crosscurrents. This volume records those currents in great detail.

In part one, the editor glances at all the musical and theatrical arts and describes their vicissitudes. The music of the Imperial Court, *gagaku,* suffered little change, even though its practitioners did at this time begin their study of Western musical instruments. Nō was the only traditional art truly threatened with extinction, for when the military shogunate that had protected it was overthrown, most of the nō schools disbanded. Had it not been for the tenacity of Umewaka Minoru, this oldest living theatre in Japan might well have died. The puppet theatre, because of its very form, was not open to great reforms, and thanks to a number of great chanters, it saw some prosperous days in the Meiji Era. Kabuki, under the influence particularly of the great actor Danjūrō IX, made efforts to become more realistic. At the same time, this master actor, especially in his later years, strove to keep the old traditions alive.

The Meiji Era saw the birth of two new theatrical forms: *shimpa,* a hybrid of Western realism and kabuki, and *shingeki,* the new theatre from the West. All the frenetic activity of this period—organization of societies, clubs, new theatres—is related at length in part two, the main body of the book, in which each of the arts, including Japanese music and dance, and Western music, is given individual treatment by a specialist.

This study is literally crammed with information, offering perhaps too much detail for the average reader. Sometimes a year-by-year, or even month-by-month, account is given of the rise and fall of theatres. Nowhere, however, will the reader find a consecutive discussion in depth of the fundamental aesthetic changes that were coming about during this important period when Japan's traditional arts were learning to face the forces of modernism and find some viable form that would be meaningful in the world of the dawning twentieth century.

7. Kusano Eisaburō. *Stories Behind Noh and Kabuki Plays.* Tokyo: Tokyo News Service, 1962. xii, 128 pp.

While this book is neither scholarly nor exhaustive, it affords enjoyable glimpses of Japan's rich folklore, which has left a strong stamp on much of its theatre. The stories told are almost all concerned with the supernatural, or at any rate, with the unusual. The historical characters described are few: Yoshitsune and Benkei, lord and retainer found invariably together in countless plays; O-Shichi, the greengrocer's daughter who set fire to Edo (Tokyo) so she might see her sweetheart; and Sen-Hime, who is here given the name the "Lady Blue Beard," although none of the adventures that earned her this sobriquet are recounted. The author fails to mention the names of the plays in which O-Shichi and Sen-Hime appear, but he does list some of the nō plays which feature Benkei and Yoshitsune.

Most of the stories deal with ghosts, demons, and such magical animals as the badger and fox which, in Japan, are able to possess and beguile human beings. Famous demons from such plays as *Modori Bridge, The Maple Viewing, The Monstrous Spider,* and *Dōjōji* are described, and the habits of other supernatural beings are explained. The author's illuminating remarks allow the reader to distinguish, should occasion arise, between an *obake* and a *yūrei,* two varieties of ghostly apparitions.

This charming and amusing book is replete with fascinating pieces of information and tales. It is also handy as a reference work, but its use in this regard is limited by the small amount of material covered and by its nonscientific approach. It is essentially a book of "Weird Tales of Old Japan," and this was indeed its original title in 1953. The present edition is slightly enlarged, and enhanced with a few references to nō and kabuki.

8. Japanese National Commission for UNESCO. *Theatre in Japan.* Paperbound. Tokyo: Printing Bureau, Ministry of Finance, 1963. 244 pp.

Compiled by outstanding Japanese authorities for the international theatre symposium in Tokyo in 1963, this small volume presents the history of Japanese theatre from the early masked dances up to the latest developments in *shingeki,* or Western forms of modern theatre, in the early 1960s. Since the material on nō and kabuki is more effectively treated in a number of other works, the value of this volume lies particularly in its sketches of twentieth-century developments in Japanese theatre. It is impossible to cover any form thoroughly in the small number of pages allotted in such publications, particularly when more than one hundred pages are given over to plot summaries which are not, in any case, complete enough to be of real aid in viewing the plays.

The chapters entitled "Modern Popular Theatre" and "The Shingeki Theatre" offer a historical outline of the various forms which developed when Japan opened to the West in the late nineteenth century. *Shimpa* and *shinkokugeki,* with its dazzling sword play, are clearly described, along with the politically oriented early shingeki and later reactions to it. The volume ends with mention of nine representative shingeki theatre groups, many of which are still performing today.

Aside from the short shrift given classical forms, this book has two major weaknesses: it eschews any critical attitudes and never becomes analytical in its approach; and its language is often too close to Japanese in its construction to allow easy reading.

9. Pronko, Leonard C. *Theater East and West: Perspectives Toward A Total Theater.* Berkeley and Los Angeles: University of California Press, 1967. 230 pp.

Contrasting the traditional oriental theatres to modern occidental theatre, the author finds that the East has a "theatre of feast," appealing to many levels, while the West thinks largely in terms of verbal theatre. In order to enlarge theatrical horizons he examines the theatres of Bali, China and Japan, describing some of the experiments with these forms that have already been made in the West, and suggesting other avenues of approach.

After treating Balinese theatre and its impact on the French visionary, Artaud, and the changing attitudes to and uses of Chinese Opera, particularly in France, he turns to the nō theatre. He divides the approaches to nō into three aspects: text, theory, performance, and concludes that, for the present, the occidental theatre would do well to explore particularly the theoretical writings of Zeami, the writer-actor-theoretician who brought nō to its peak in the late fourteenth century.

Obviously most impressed by the theatrical possibilities of kabuki, the author describes early twentieth-century contacts between kabuki and the West, then makes specific suggestions of how use of kabuki techniques might benefit occidental theatre. He describes in some detail American productions of kabuki, and in particular an experiment treating Marlowe's *Jew of Malta* in kabuki terms.

A final chapter attempts to sum up the characteristics of oriental theatre, describing it with three adjectives: participative, total, stylized. A useful bibliography is appended, and sixteen pages of photographs help the reader to visualize the theatres described.

10. Arnott, Peter D. *The Theatres of Japan.* New York: St. Martin's Press, 1969. 319 pp.

This superb study of the major theatrical forms of Japan, including the most modern, offers a splendid introduction. At the same time, it is a study in depth of certain aesthetic and philosophical questions connected with theatre in general, and Japanese theatre in particular. After a quick glance at Japan's history, the author (a respected scholar of Greek theatre and drama, and a well-known puppeteer) plunges the reader into the atmosphere of dance and festival as he discusses the origins of Japan's theatrical arts.

The chapter on nō, drawing on vast erudition and no little philosophical acumen, does a good deal more than discuss the history and performance of the austere classical drama. Professor Arnott goes beyond the form and the text (to which he also does justice) in order to treat the spirit which animates the plays and dictates their form. Never does abstraction win out, however, for every point is illustrated concretely, and many plays are described in detail. The kyōgen (comic interludes) are given their due and a number of them recounted.

Throughout, Arnott suggests helpful analogies with Greek, Elizabethan, and other forms of Western threatre. The chapter on kabuki contrasts this popular form to the aristocratic nō, evokes a colorful performance of the masterpiece *Sukeroku*, and in a fascinating and highly original passage, suggests similarities between kabuki's structure and that of the Japanese language itself.

In the chapter entitled "Puppet, Mask, Costume, Actor," Arnott describes the puppets, compares them with kabuki performers, and in a brilliant passage compares the aesthetics of representational theatre (such as realism and naturalism which have dominated the modern West) with that of presentational theatre (like traditional Asian forms, or Greek and Elizabethan theatre), suggesting the social and philosophical attitudes which lead to each. As always, the author is judicious, unbiased, and uses numerous concrete examples to make his points. Throughout the book he generalizes from the particular instances under discussion, thus giving his work a much broader interest than simply that of a study of Japanese theatre: he is talking about the very concept of theatre and its many ways of dealing with reality.

The last chapter treats modern theatre, largely through perceptive reviews of productions the author had seen, ranging from Greek tragedy in Japanese dress *(Oedipus at Hiroshima)*, through Pirandello and Tolstoi, to modern musicals and the all-girl Takarazuka review (which he mistakenly calls new kabuki). Several appendices are included: particularly interesting is the one which compares three productions of the same play, *Shunkan*, in nō, puppet and kabuki versions.

The first book to consider at length the philosophy and aesthetics of the whole of Japanese theatre in the broad context of world theatre, *Theatres of Japan* is a landmark. It will be profitably consulted by the beginner, but deserves even more the serious study of mature theatre specialists.

General Works: Anthologies

11. Keene, Donald, ed. *Anthology of Japanese Literature: From the Earliest Era to the Mid-Nineteenth Century.* New York: Grove Press, 1955. 442 pp. (Paperback, Evergreen Books).

12. Keene, Donald, ed. *Modern Japanese Literature: An Anthology.* New York: Grove Press, 1956. 440 pp. (Paperback, Evergreen Books).

The richness and variety of the material devoted to theatre in volume one of this anthology (76 pages: 9 passages by 5 or 6 authors) compared with the paucity of material in volume two (24 pages: 2 items by 2 authors) is no doubt an indication of the weak state of modern theatre in Japan in contrast to the wealth of traditional forms which flourished before the Meiji Restoration (1868).

While a number of excerpts in the first volume will furnish background for understanding some of the major themes used in Japanese theatre (for example, the selections from the old chanted epic tales of the Heike), those which deal specifically with the theatre are centered on nō and kyōgen in the Muromachi period (1333–1600) and puppet drama in the Tokugawa (1600–1868). Two valuable passages by the master of the nō form, Zeami, discuss fundamental principles of that difficult art, and particularly the concept of *yūgen*. A diagram of the nō stage precedes the texts of four important nō plays: *Sotoba Komachi*, *Birds of Sorrow (Utō)*, *Atsumori*, and *The Damask Drum (Aya no tsuzumi)*, the last two reprinted from Waley's *The Nō Plays of Japan* (no. **30**). Two delightful kyōgen, or comic interludes to the nō performance, follow: *The Bird-Catcher in Hades (Esashi Jūō)* and *Busu*.

The puppet theatre is represented by two writings of Chikamatsu, usually considered the finest of all Japanese dramatists. His reported words, "On the Art of the Puppet Stage," are justly famous and contain the oft quoted lines defining art as "something which lies in the slender margin between the real and the unreal." The full text of *The Love Suicides at Sonezaki* in Keene's sensitive translation is included. It is one of Chikamatsu's shorter plays, but also one of his finest, and contains the magnificent poetry of the *michiyuki*, or travel scene, as the two lovers journey toward death.

Compared with these rewarding texts, the two plays in volume two seem very dry, but they are typical of the periods in which they were written and reveal the influence of Western theatre and the realism prevalent at the time. Kawatake Mokuami is considered the greatest kabuki playwright of the nineteenth century, but the final act of *The Thieves* (1881) has none of the charm, richness, poetry or theatricality of Chikamatsu's lovely piece. Coincidence, sudden conversion, and virtue triumphant are no doubt more convincing in the theatre when coupled with dramatic poses, but as text they will strike the reader as sentimental and melodramatic. Kikuchi Kan's *Madman on the Roof* (1916) possesses a certain wistful charm, but is not much more than a brief vignette of island life in 1900.

13. Ernst, Earle, ed. *Three Japanese Plays from the Traditional Theatre.* London and New York: Oxford University Press, 1959. xv, 200 pp. (Paperback, Grove Press, Evergreen Books).

This edition of three outstanding adaptations of well-known plays from the nō, puppet, and kabuki theatres will be useful both for reading and for production. The translations are eminently playable and are supplied with stage directions. Each of the three plays is preceded by a concise and enlightening introduction which touches upon all essentials.

The nō play, *The Maple Viewing* (which was adapted for kabuki at the end of the nineteenth century), is a poetic rendering of the tale of the warrior Koremochi. While hunting in the forest, he comes upon a beautiful young lady who is viewing the maple leaves. She invites him to join her, dances for him, and finally induces slumber through drink. When he is asleep, she disappears and returns in her true shape as a demon. The god of the mountain wakens him, and he fights and kills the demon.

The puppet play, *The House of Sugawara (Sugawara Denju Tenarai Kagami),* is one of the three most famous doll plays of the history type, and some scenes are constantly played either by the puppets or by the kabuki actors in whose repertoire the play is also immensely popular. It narrates the vicissitudes of a number of characters attached to the family or household of the great Lord Sugawara who, through the machinations of the evil minister, Shihei, is exiled. Scenes of humor and bombast alternate with those of more gentle sentiments, reaching a climax in the moving (and most famous) scene of act 3, known as "Terakoya" or "The Village School," in which Lord Matsuomaru sacrifices his own son to save the son of his lord.

The kabuki piece is representative of the raw domestic play which was the specialty of the greatest kabuki dramatist of the nineteenth century, Kawatake Mokuami. *Benten the Thief,* blending all the typical beauties and splendors of kabuki in a story which is compelling, comical, and sometimes moving, relates the adventures of five notorious thieves.

This volume is a major contribution to the literature of Japanese theatre in English and offers texts of immediate appeal. The doll and kabuki plays were used for performances at the University of Hawaii and are called "versions" rather than "translations," for they were adapted to the requirements of Western theatrical needs. While not always literally faithful, they retain the spirit and vitality of the original in a way that might not have been possible in a more literal rendering.

14. Anderson, George L., ed. *The Genius of the Oriental Theater.* Paperbound. New York and Toronto: New American Library, Mentor Books, 1966. 416 pp.

About half this volume is devoted to two lengthy Indian plays, and the rest to Japanese theatre. A succinct introduction to the nō theatre outlines the history of the form and its distinctive features as performance and as literature. Although the comic interludes (kyōgen) are mentioned, unfortunately no examples are included in the anthology. The six nō plays are taken from

Waley's volume (no. **30**), and are arranged in a cycle so that the reader can imagine the rhythm of a traditional program.

The brief introduction to the kabuki and *jōruri* (puppet theatre) is concerned chiefly with helping the reader to appreciate the Chikamatsu text that follows. It gives him the necessary background regarding eighteenth-century society, the stylization of the puppets, and the major techniques and themes used by this major Japanese dramatist. The puppet play included is *The Courier for Hell* in a superlative translation by Donald Keene (see no. **60**). It recounts the story of a hero, good but rash, who breaks the seal on money entrusted to him in order to prove to his enemies that he can afford to buy out of bondage the courtesan he loves. To save his honor, he is forced to flee. In one of those scenes largely made up of dance, he voyages to his hometown to say farewell to his father, before killing himself together with his sweetheart. In this original version the couple are apprehended before they can kill themselves, but in later adaptations for the kabuki, they are allowed to die as the curtain falls.

Kabuki is represented by A. C. Scott's translation of *The Subscription List (Kanjinchō,* see no. **59**), one of the supreme masterpieces of the kabuki stage. The text includes a good many details of the movement, which enable the reader to visualize to some extent the staging which, more than the text, is the glory of this drama.

Although all of these texts are available elsewhere, this book brings together a sampling of various kinds of Japanese drama and presents them in an organized fashion at a very reasonable price.

15. Brandon, James R., ed. *Traditional Asian Plays.* New York: Hill and Wang, Mermaid Dramabook, 1972. 308 pp. (Paperback).

This excellent collection, containing Indian, Thai, and Chinese works as well as Japanese, "is designed to suggest to the reader, and the prospective theatre director, a total theatrical experience." Since traditional theatres of the orient are without exception meant to be performed rather than read, such an approach is not only justifiable, but devoutly to be wished. As oriental texts become more familiar and more available in the West, Brandon's format will no doubt be followed with greater frequency. All of the plays as translated and described in this volume have been performed in the United States by American actors or students.

The terse introductions to nō and kabuki are models of their kind, presenting precisely the information most essential to an understanding and appreciation of the text as theatre. The origin and production of each play is succinctly described in short introductions before each script. The nō play, *Ikkaku Sennin,* is given in a text originally translated by Frank Hoff and then arranged by William Packard into syllabic patterns identical to the original for performance at the Institute for Advanced Studies in the Theatre Arts. *Ikkaku Sennin* is the story of a hermit priest who is seduced by a court lady in order to free the rain gods he has imprisoned. In the usual nō manner, understatement and faint suggestion prevail, except in the final dance, where the priest-turned-demon expresses his wrath.

The kabuki texts, translated by Brandon and Niwa Tamako for production at the University of Michigan, are *The Subscription List (Kanjinchō)* and *The Zen Substitute (Migawari Zazen)* (available separately, see Further Reading), both popular items in the present-day kabuki repertoire. The first, considered one of the sublime masterpieces of kabuki, is a dance play based on the nō play *Ataka,* recounting how Benkei, the loyal retainer, saves the life of his lord, Yoshitsune, by clever subterfuge. The play is theatrically brilliant and deeply moving. *The Zen Substitute,* adapted from a kyōgen, the comic interlude to nō, relates an amusing story of marital infidelity, much of it presented in dance form.

All the texts in this volume are highly playable, and contain detailed descriptions of movement, props and costumes. They present a high standard against which to measure future publications of theatre texts.

16. Irwin, Vera R., ed. *Four Classical Asian Plays.* Paperbound. Baltimore, Maryland: Penguin, Pelican Books, 1972. 333 pp.

The greater part of this book consists of two lengthy plays, one from India and the other from China. But the two Japanese plays are of great interest because they represent the same story as embodied first in a nō play and then in the kabuki. The story of the hermit seduced by a lovely woman intent on discovering the secret of releasing the rain gods he has imprisoned is treated in the nō play *Ikkaku Sennin* and the kabuki play *Narukami*.

Ikkaku Sennin is preceded by a dense introduction which traces the history and aesthetic background of nō, including technical details of music and form not usually found in an introductory work. The text, originally translated by Frank Hoff, was rendered by William Packard into the identical syllable count of the Japanese for its production at the Institute for Advanced Studies in the Theatre Arts in New York. The text is followed by production notes by Mr. Packard, stressing the discipline required by the movement and rhythms of the nō form.

The introduction to *Narukami* briefly traces the history of kabuki and emphasizes its theatricality as contrasted to the subtlety of the nō. It goes on to explain the origin of the play and its theatrical effectiveness by evoking highlights from its performance. The text of this flamboyant play, adapted by Watanabe Miyoko, was used for performances at the Institute for Advanced Studies in the Theatre Arts. Miss Watanabe's production comments draw on this experience as well as on her vast knowledge of kabuki techniques.

Good critical apparatus makes this an effective introduction to nō and kabuki, while the comparison rendered possible by the inclusion of two plays dealing with the same theme will help to emphasize those characteristics which are typical of each of these highly individual theatrical forms.

Nō and Kyōgen: Criticism

*(See also nos. **1, 2, 3, 6,** and **8–10**.)*

17. Nogami Toyoichirō. *Noh Plays: How to See Them.* Paper-bound. Tokyo: Nōgaku Shorin, 1954. 76 pp.

This small book, intended for the foreigner who wishes to understand what he sees at the nō theatre, was one of the first of its kind. Like most books with a similar purpose, it discusses, in order, the structure of the theatre, the elements of performance, and the masks and costumes. Photographs accompany each topic discussed, and the chapter on performance is made concrete by brief descriptions of two plays being performed.

The author goes into some detail on classifications of nō plays, and then treats the organization of an entire program, both in traditional terms of five plays, and in contemporary practice of two or three. He advises the spectator to determine whether the play he is viewing is chiefly to be seen or to be heard, so that he may know what to expect and how to appreciate it best.

The most interesting, because the most unusual, chapter is the final one entitled simply "Repertoire," in which the author lists some one hundred fifty most popular plays according to the major theme or attraction of each play. For example, listed are pieces in which the major features are respectively, the tragic death of an old warrior, the dance of a supernatural female being, a man's madness, and sword-fighting.

The Foreword possesses a curious interest for its mention of such famous Westerners as G.B. Shaw and Paul Claudel, who viewed nō under Professor Nogami's tutelage. Shaw's reaction, while not particularly "Shavian," is reported at some length. The book is illustrated with clear photographs and a detailed diagram of the nō stage.

18. Toki Zemmaro. *Japanese Nō Plays.* Tokyo: Japan Travel Bureau, 1954. 204 pp.

This compact and informative book may be divided into three large sections: aesthetics, performance, and classification. In simple language the author attempts to elucidate the many elements of this complex and subtle art, which dates from six hundred years ago. Under such headings as "characteristic elements," "quintessence," "main object," and "ultimate aim," he deals with such concepts as elegance, nobility, dignity, beauty, subtlety, and suggestivity, and explains the principle of *jo, ha, kyū* (introduction, development, finale) which regulates the nō structure and performance. He also briefly traces the history of nō.

The stage, theatre, costumes, and masks, described in some detail, are illustrated by abundant photographs and a few drawings. The staging of the plays is rendered more vivid by a detailed description of two plays, accompanied by photographs which take the actor from his costuming backstage to his arrival on the platform before the audience. The roles of *mai* (dance or acting), *utai* (rhythmic chant) and *hayashi* (stage orchestra) are treated. Finally, the reader is made aware of the various elements that need to be observed in a performance in order to enhance his appreciation. The literary aspects of the texts, which Toki rightly claims are not essential to an appreciation of the nō performance, are quickly outlined.

Synopses of twenty-six popular nō plays are given in detail, and many of them illustrated with photographs. On the whole, this book forms an excellent introduction to nō both through its text and its many photographs.

19. O'Neill, Patrick G. *A Guide to Nō*. Tokyo and Kyoto: Hinoki Shoten, 1955. 229 pp.

This practical little book is intended primarily for students of the nō who have the opportunity to see performances and wish to have an outline of the stories to follow. For a volume of minuscule dimensions, it contains an amazing amount of information. A terse introduction presents the essentials for an understanding of nō's history, its organization, elements of performance, and fundamental aesthetics. Naturally, it takes more than a few pages to deal with these subjects thoroughly; nevertheless, O'Neill, with an outstanding scholarly background of investigation into the high period of nō, is able to suggest the important outlines of each.

Most of the book is of course filled with concise outlines of the plots of the plays—including some 240 works currently in the repertoires of the nō theatres—arranged, for easy reference, in alphabetical order. Each outline is preceded by the title in both Roman letters and Japanese characters, the author's name, the group to which the play belongs by virtue of its subject and treatment, the schools which today perform the play, and a list of characters. A diagram and photograph of the stage, and clear line drawings of important stage properties, hats, fans and masks, help the reader to understand such items when they are used in performance.

While this tiny (6" × 3½") tome is intended primarily to be popped into purse or pocket before leaving for the nō theatre, it is also a very handy reference work.

20. Nogami Toyoichirō. *Zeami and His Theories on Noh.* Tr. by Matsumoto Ryōzō. Tokyo: Hinoki Shoten, 1955. 89 pp.

This volume represents the first effort to deal at some length in English with the ideas expressed in the *Kadensho*, a document sometimes called the "Bible" of nō, written by the man who is universally acknowledged to have brought nō to its highest degree of achievement, Zeami. In two introductory chapters Professor Nogami deals with early developments in the nō, and the contributions of Kannami and his son Zeami which led nō to occupy its preeminent position. A convenient listing of all Zeami's writings, in presumed chronological order, is given. The central chapters of the book take up Zeami's principal ideas under four major headings: *monomane* (imitation), *yūgen* (transcendental phantasm), *hana* (flower), and *ran-i* (attained skill). These mysterious expressions are elucidated briefly by the author, and although some questions are cleared up, others remain opaque. Particularly troublesome is the concept of *yūgen*, which within this book receives four or five different translations without much probing into the development of that concept in Zeami's mind.

The last chapter treats the stages of training of the nō actor, age by age, and ends with a wise admonition to the nō artists of today, reminding them that traditional arts must adapt to modern man's sensibilities while remaining faithful to the essence of what Zeami taught.

This book, while a bit dated and sometimes rendered in an English that is not idiomatic, still offers the beginning reader an organized approach to the ideas of nō's major theoretician.

21. O'Neill, Patrick G. *Early No Drama: Its Background, Character and Development, 1300–1450.* London: Lund Humphries, 1958. 223 pp.

The period covered by *Early No Drama* is the most vital in the history of this theatrical form, and as such is essential to an understanding of what nō is today, and what it was intended to be. The author discusses the dramatic forms which preceded the nō, focusing on the two out of which nō developed, *sarugaku* and *dengaku*. With great clarity and admirable use of detail, Professor O'Neill paints a total picture of the conditions surrounding the creation and performance of these works in the fourteenth century, reminding us that the aristocratic form of today derives from popular entertainment.

In tracing the history of this entertainment, he draws on documents of the period and chiefly upon the writings of Zeami, considered the greatest figure in the history of nō, both for his plays and his theoretical works. It was Zeami's father, Kannami, who first brought together sarugaku and another popular form of musical entertainment known as *kuse mai*, thus creating what we today call nō. O'Neill treats this question, like all others, with scholarly precision and care, but never pedantically. He authoritatively establishes the importance of kuse mai in the development of nō, and analyzes its particular qualities.

After carefully constructing a picture of Kannami, and outlining his contributions, he goes on to the better-known figure of Zeami, whose lifetime corresponds to the zenith of nō's development.

Those who are acquainted with nō performances today tend to see it exclusively as a restrained and highly ceremonious form of theatre. *Early No Drama* is a healthy corrective to this one-sided view: O'Neill describes nō as it was performed not only for the aesthetes of the reigning shogunal court but for the public both in the cities and in the countryside. Citing contemporary documents, he effectively evokes the somewhat rough-and-tumble atmosphere of public performances in the fifteenth century and traces the development of the physical stage. After studying the content of programs and their usual length, he concludes that nō plays performed in the fifteenth century lasted only about half the time the same plays take to be performed today.

Zeami's contribution to theatrical aesthetics is of no little importance. Unfortunately, his treatises have not been translated in their entirety. This book offers perceptive insights and sensitive interpretations for the reader interested in understanding this important aspect of nō. The development of music, dance, text, and aesthetic attitudes is chronicled in a precise but lively way.

Appendices offer lists of nō plays written before Zeami's time, those written by Zeami, and valuable translations of two *dengaku nō* plays and two plays belonging to the kuse mai tradition.

This book forms a solid base for subsequent study, but is perhaps best approached after some more general introductory reading in the field; although written with the utmost precision and clarity, it is dense with ideas and information, a rich diet for one unaccustomed to such feasting.

22. Upton, Murakami, Mr. and Mrs. *A Spectator's Handbook of Noh.* Tokyo: Wanya Shoten, Japan Publications Company, 1963. x, 97 pp.

Although a bit large for pocket or purse, this volume is intended primarily for the student who is about to view a nō presentation. It contains, in summary form, the essentials for an appreciation of the nō. A brief introduction deals with elements of performance, structure of the plays and their classification. Two pages of photographs help identify the various masks which may be used, and a drawing of the stage acquaints the neophyte with peculiarities of its structure. But the substance of the book lies in its summaries of about fifty plays in the current repertoire. A page or two is devoted to each summary, and numerous photographs, as well as occasional drawings of major stage properties, are included. The summary usually gives background information and translations of several major passages, a few notes, and reference to other plays which treat the same theme or use the same major character.

In addition to the summaries of major plays, there are thirty-eight brief synopses, and a number of one-line descriptions of shrine nō plays and those that pertain to mythological or supernatural characters. Literary sources for the plays are noted, a map of central Japan shows the location of most of the places mentioned in the play summaries, and a character-title index refers the reader to the proper synopsis.

While this handbook is neither as scholarly nor as thorough as O'Neill's *Guide to Nō* (no. **19**), to which it admits its indebtedness, it is attractively presented, and the many photos add to its usefulness in helping the novice to relate masks, costumes and poses to specific plays.

23. Keene, Donald. *Nō: The Classical Theatre of Japan.* Photographs by Kaneko Hiroshi. Tokyo and Palo Alto: Kōdansha International, 1966. 314 pp.

This authoritative and substantial study of nō by one of the outstanding American scholars of Japanese literature is as impressive in size and physical beauty as it is in depth and comprehensiveness. Like the Kōdansha publications devoted to kabuki and bunraku, this large (10″ × 14″) volume features almost 200 pages of color and black-and-white photographs. The text forms an excellent introduction to the art, but takes the reader much further than do the usual introductory works.

It is studded with original insights and statements, and presents an immense amount of new material not before available in English.

An opening chapter introduces the reader to "the pleasures of nō," essaying a definition of this elusive theatrical form and outlining its major aesthetic elements. The important concepts of Zeami, the major figure in bringing nō to its highest point of development, are discussed in some detail, particularly the concept of *yūgen* in all its complex and shifting meanings from "grace" and "charm" to some ineffable mystical feeling. Due attention is also paid to the kyōgen, the delightful comic interludes performed between the several nō plays of a full-length program.

The longest chapter, on the history of nō and kyōgen, traces in sharp, clear lines the development of the form from its earliest manifestations up to the present. It is of particular interest to read of nō's development after the period of Zeami because this is rarely treated although of immense importance for an understanding of nō as it exists today and for an understanding of nō's influence on the popular theatre in Japan. Its popularity with the common people as late as the sixteenth century, its growth in the direction of a popular entertainment, and its freezing into the official form of ritual under the Tokugawa regime are all vividly described.

In the chapter concerned with nō and kyōgen as literature, Professor Keene lucidly writes about the technical aspects of versification and poetic technique, and traces the decadence of nō poetry in later works. He buttresses his statements with many examples, always rooting his discussion in the precise reality of specific plays and performances. In the remaining chapters the stage, properties, performance, and musical elements are elucidated with rare understanding and precision.

The photographs begin with a rich series of 115 pictures illustrating a full program of nō and kyōgen, surely the best introduction to a nō program short of viewing an actual performance. Captions are fully explanatory and direct the reader's attention to significant details. Pictures of historic nō, and regional versions of nō and kyōgen follow. Forty-six pages are devoted to superb photographs, many in color, of the masks which are a treasured element of nō and kyōgen. After gorgeous color photos of costumes and fans, a selection of shots that depict the vocabulary of gestures and illustrations of various elements of staging, the photo section ends with 55 pages of dramatic photographs from selected nō and kyōgen performances.

Appended to the work proper are a list of nō plays currently performed, a bibliography, four pages of line drawings showing major roles and their costumes, and a small recording of scenes from a famous nō play, *Funa Benkei* (Benkei on the Boat), with accompanying text in Japanese and English.

This impressive book will no doubt for many years remain the definitive English language study of nō and kyōgen.

24. Kenny, Don. *A Guide to Kyōgen.* Tokyo: Hinoki Shoten, 1968. 303 pp.

The author of this work, drama critic for the *Japan Times*, film actor, translator of a number of books in this bibliography, and for many years a student of the Nomura Kyōgen group, is well suited to his task. After a brief introduction by the well-known writer on Japanese film, Donald Richie, in which the warmth and humor of kyōgen are aptly evoked, Kenny presents a few prefatory comments to help the reader understand the background of the kyōgen form. His description of the costumes peculiar to various character types will be particularly helpful to the novice when he attends the plays.

Essentially this volume, like any guide book, is meant to be taken in hand while one views the material covered. There are rather detailed synopses of the 257 plays in the current repertoire of the two still existent schools of kyōgen, arranged, for easy reference, in alphabetical order. Each synopsis is preceded by the play's title in Roman letters, Japanese characters, and in English translation; an indication of which school or schools perform the play; and a list of the characters. Many of the plays are illustrated by charming line drawings with an archaic air, showing the major characters engaged in conversation or action on the nō stage where these comic interludes are still performed as part of the normal nō program.

While the volume is primarily for the theatregoer, it makes enchanting reading simply for the wit and charm of the stories, which recount the universal foolishness of mankind. Despite several visits of kyōgen troupes to this country, the kyōgen is still not widely known. This book will help the reader realize the breadth of its repertoire and the immediate appeal of its themes.

25. Zeami Motokiyo. *Kadensho.* Tr. by Sakurai Chūichi, Hayashi Shūseki, Satoi Rokurō, and Miyai Bin. Kyoto: Sumiya Shinobe Publishing Institute, 1968. 109 pp. (Distr. by Japan Publications Trading Co., San Francisco).

The *Kadensho* is one of the most important treatises by Zeami, at once supreme author, actor and theoretician, the man responsible for bringing the nō to its peak of perfection. This honest and readable translation offers English readers the opportunity, within the limits of a translated work, to interpret for themselves many of the fundamental ideas underlying nō as it was understood at its zenith. An intelligent introduction points out the major ideas of the treatise and relates them to those contained in other works by Zeami.

The *Kadensho* reflects Zeami's training under his brilliant father Kannami, whom he idolized, and offers us today a fascinating picture of nō before it had congealed into the official "music" of the shogunate. In his introduction Zeami stresses the importance for the actor to lead a pure and disciplined life, thus suggesting the spirituality of nō in its highest reaches, a theme to which he will return near the end of this essay.

An initial chapter is devoted to the proper training for each age in life, ending with the subdued plays recommended for the actor over fifty who "had better do nothing." Here, and in the following chapters, Zeami discusses such vital principles as the *hana* (lit., flower, perhaps "charm appropriate to each age" is the closest definition), *monomane* or the representation of reality, and *yūgen* (perhaps best rendered as "elegance" or "profound beauty").

One is constantly aware that Zeami is a man of the theatre in the fullest sense of the word, conscious of the importance of pleasing his audience, at whatever level, and even of making ends meet financially. Writing for a nō theatre that was still vital and changing, he advises his actor to adapt himself to conditions of performance, to perform often in plays of his own composition, and to be certain that his movements accompany the words and melody meaningfully. Actors, play, and audience, are constantly taken into account.

This fascinating document has more than a historical interest; it offers even today rich insights into dramatic art, and may be studied by modern nō actor and Western student alike. Regarding the *Kadensho* one is tempted to give the same advice Zeami repeatedly gave his actors: "You had better ponder it deeply."

Presented in a small, handsome format, this extremely valuable book is illustrated with eight large, clear, artistically rendered photographs of masks and scenes from plays.

26. Maruoka Daiji, and Yoshikoshi Tatsuo. *Noh.* Tr. by Don Kenny. Hoikusha Color Books. Paperbound. Osaka: Hoikusha Publishing Co., 1969. 127 pp.

Only in Japan could a book of such tiny format be so lavishly illustrated with vivid color photographs and yet sell at such a modest price. Like the other books in this series, which range from gem stones to goldfish, this small (4" × 6") volume is replete with exciting photographs, astonishingly clear for their small size. Every other page features pictures in color, while alternating pages are filled with black-and-white shots. Each of the 96 pages of photographs is devoted to a major play of the repertoire and is accompanied by a brief recounting of the story. In orderly fashion, the plays are arranged according to the five groups as traditionally presented.

The final thirty pages are made up of text describing the physical structure of the nō theatre in great detail, and summary descriptions of elements of performance, costumes, plays, actors, and so forth. While the text does not pretend to be comprehensive, it is as detailed as limited space will allow. For a modest sum, this book offers an inviting introduction to the visual sumptuousness and rich repertoire of the nō.

27. Nakamura Yasuo. *Noh: The Classical Theater*. Tr. by Don Kenny. Performing Arts of Japan, no. 4. New York, Tokyo and Kyoto: Weatherhill/Tankosha, 1971. 248 pp.

Like the other volumes of the Performing Arts of Japan series, this one is handsomely presented, with many pages of glorious color photographs and dramatic black-and-white ones. This volume features a detailed pictorial history of the nō and its many antecedent dances and theatrical forms. The introduction by Earle Ernst is lively and enlightening with personal reminiscences of his contacts with Japanese theatre during the Occupation. He establishes analogies with Western theatre that render the difficult nō more comprehensible to the novice. Too, he does not slight the comic interludes or kyōgen which are omitted or only lightly touched upon in many studies of nō including the present volume.

Professor Nakamura's first chapter, "Noh as Stage Art," briefly describes some aspects of the nō performance, and serves as an introduction to the real marrow of his book, which is a rather detailed historical exploration of the development of nō throughout the centuries. Much of his material is new in English, and all of it is of interest to the aficionado of nō in search of a deeper understanding of this complex art. Nakamura stresses quite rightly the number of changes that have taken place in nō since its highest point of development in the days of Zeami, almost six hundred years ago. Following its vicissitudes during a brief period of vulgarization, and then into the formalization under the Tokugawas (1600–1868), he describes certain innovations made within the last century.

A final chapter deals with "Noh Today," taking up such questions as training, masks, costumes, properties, music, movement, and the performance. Some of the photographs supplement this most effectively, including a series showing basic poses and their meanings. The final section leads us back full circle to the beginning, where the author had quoted the contemporary French playwright Ionesco: "Noh is avant-garde theatre." Like many others today, Nakamura believes that nō has much to offer the West, and that the nō actors themselves may contribute toward a revitalization of this form that is rich in possibilities for modern man.

28. Inoura Yoshinobu. *A History of Japanese Theater I: Up to Noh and Kyogen.* Paperbound. Tokyo: Kokusai Bunka Shinkōkai, 1971. 163 pp.

This admirably organized study of early Japanese theatre and the gradual development of nō, is a detailed presentation, both historical and critical, of the forms that have contributed to the rich theatrical heritage of Japan. A brief introduction presents an overview of the subject, and is followed in the first section by chapters which treat the individual forms. More than in any other volume, the student will find here a wealth of background on the earliest forms and many varieties of *kagura, bugaku, gigaku,* and the later forms which contributed so importantly to the development of nō: *sarugaku, dengaku, ennen nō,* and *shūgen nō.* Each chapter, a model of clarity, begins with a section on the history of the form, dividing it into its major periods when this is feasible, and stressing the contributions of each.

A second section treats the performance, the kinds of plays included and the composition of the programs. The chapter describing nō itself will give the student many insights into the varied forms which evolved into the nō of today, passing through the important period of consolidation under Kannami, Zeami and Zenchiku, a period of change, and the final period of stabilization under the Tokugawas.

The comic interludes, kyōgen, are not overlooked, and their development is constantly related to that of nō itself. The description of the nō performances today is the least original part of the book, but rounds out the information essential to an understanding of the form.

A final chapter takes up briefly the possibility of Chinese influence on the early theatre forms. Helpful appendices list the repertoires of bugaku, nō and kyōgen, and sixteen pages of photos add effective visual aids to the text.

Simple and clear and based on sound scholarship, this is a thorough and satisfying study.

Nō and Kyōgen: Texts

(See also nos. **11** *and* **13–16.***)*

29. Pound, Ezra, and Fenollosa, Ernest, trs. *The Classic Noh Theatre of Japan.* (Originally published in the United States as *'Noh' or Accomplishment: A Study of the Classical Stage of Japan,* 1917). Paperbound. New York: New Directions, 1959. 163 pp.

This slim volume is of immense historical interest, for it is one of the landmarks in the introduction of Japanese theatre to the West. Fenollosa, one of the great exponents of Japanese culture at the end of the nineteenth century, left notes and skeletal translations among his papers at his death, and Pound gave them this publishable form. First published privately in Dublin in 1916 as *Certain Noble Plays of Japan,* these translations exercised a profound influence upon William Butler Yeats.

New discoveries relating to the history of nō, and strides in aesthetic appreciation of this highly refined theatre have been made since Pound wrote his work in 1916, but essentially he appears to have had a deep understanding of its spirit and its form. In fact, Pound the aesthetic Imagist is perhaps too ready to admit uncritically everything admirable that can be attributed to the nō, and the modern student is well advised to read with a critical eye and correct his impressions from this book with a dose of more modern, objective scholarship.

The book is divided into four sections without any apparent rationale behind these divisions; plays of differing types are given in each, frequently with many deletions. The brevity of these cut versions gives a mistaken impression, but certainly renders reading relatively easy, particularly in the often lovely adaptations made by Pound.

The fifteen or so plays are set within a framework of Pound's commentary and the transcriptions of interviews and other notes which Fenollosa derived from his firsthand contact with the world of nō actors during the twenty years he studied nō singing and dancing. Chapter 3 is a lengthy article by Fenollosa in which he details the history of nō, comparing it with other Japanese and Chinese arts, and studies its literary aspects. This chapter, as well as the introduction which Yeats wrote for the 1916 Irish edition, and which the editors have thoughtfully included in this volume, make for fascinating and illuminating reading.

30. Waley, Arthur, tr. *The Nō Plays of Japan*. (1921). Paperbound. New York: Grove Press, Evergreen Books, 1957. 319 pp.

The first scholarly book in English to tackle the nō, this remains one of the finest introductions to the subject. Waley's reputation as the father of Japanese literary studies and translations in English rests upon a solid knowledge of both Chinese and Japanese, an encyclopedic understanding, and a command of the English language that allowed him to render sensitively the poetic nuances of the original.

A substantial introduction opens the volume, acquainting the reader with the background and historical development of the nō and dealing at length, for the first time in English, with Kannami and Zeami, the two most important figures in the development of the form. The latter's writings form the backbone of nō and reveal much about the early period of its development. They are still not translated into English in their entirety, but Waley gives translations of large portions and summarizes other sections: particularly when read along with Waley's sensitive and sometimes witty comments, there is enough to give the reader an understanding of the essential points. He devotes an interesting page or two to Webster's *Duchess of Malfi* as it might be performed in a nō version, thus giving the newcomer from the West a means of access through a relatively familiar dramatic work.

The bulk of the book is devoted to translations of nō plays, usually grouped thematically, and prefaced by a few notes regarding the characters or historical background. The texts themselves are accompanied by notes explaining allusions, but there has been no attempt to incorporate the complexities of

Japanese poetic techniques into the English versions. A penultimate chapter sums up sixteen plays, with very brief excerpts of a few important passages, and the final chapter is a translation of one kyōgen or farcical interlude included in the standard nō program.

Two appendices are of interest: one describes modern performances of nō (1916) largely as seen through the eyes of an astute and sensitive observer whose letters are quoted at length; the other itemizes "some of the facts brought to light by the discovery of Seami's *Works.*"

Waley's book is half a century old, but of abiding interest and value for its scholarly insights and the beauty of his translations.

31. Sakanishi Shio, tr. *Japanese Folk-Plays: The Ink-Smeared Lady and Other Kyōgen.* (1938). Rutland, Vermont and Tokyo: Charles E. Tuttle Co., 1960. (Paperback).

The twenty-two kyōgen in this volume give a broad sampling of the delightful comic interludes which were traditionally performed between the more austere nō plays. Like the nō, the kyōgen are highly stylized in performance, but they are much more human and poke fun at the foibles and foolishness of noble and commoner, man and woman alike.

A substantial introduction discusses the development of the kyōgen and its association with the nō. The genius who brought nō to its full flower, Zeami, treated kyōgen in his theoretical works, and some of these remarks are included here. The sources and aesthetic values of these short folk plays are treated, and the physicality of their comedy, which most often depends on situation, is underlined.

The plays treat many themes. *The Ink-Smeared Lady* reveals the insincerity of a lord's mistress whose false tears of farewell are exposed when the clever servant-boy replaces a water bottle with an inkwell. *Busu* shows the lord outwitted by his crafty servants: leaving precious sugar in their care at home, the lord warns them not even to go near it because it is poisonous. Their curiosity getting the better of them, they finally consume the sugar. Then in order to excuse themselves, they destroy the master's art treasures and, upon his return, claim that they had tried to commit suicide by eating the "poison" after accidentally ruining the treasures.

Friendly demons, greedy old people, deceitful servants, gullible gods, stupid lords, simple-minded acolytes people this entertaining world. The warm humor of the plays, which will appeal to readers of all backgrounds, shines delightfully in these sprightly translations.

A comprehensive list of kyōgen translations in English is appended and adds to the usefulness of this volume.

32. Nippon Gakujutsu Shinkōkai, tr. *Japanese Noh Drama: Ten Plays Selected and Translated from the Japanese.* 3 vols. Rutland, Vermont and Tokyo: Charles E. Tuttle Co., 1955–60. xvi, 182; xxvi, 178; and xxviii, 192 pp.

These three volumes, each containing ten plays, are the result of many years of labor by a group of outstanding Japanese scholars. Although there has been no effort to remain faithful to the original rhythms or to incorporate all the literary devices of the original into the English versions, these translations are impressive—they are not only readable, they are accurate and poetically appealing.

Each volume contains an introduction; the three read in order give an excellent background to the nō. The first deals in a general way with the structure of the stage, the roles, order of the plays, and their style and classification. The second covers in detail the properties used by the nō actor, including costume, wigs, headdress, masks, and stage props. The third treats at length the texts, their composition, sources, aesthetics, and classification.

Each play is in turn preceded by an introduction relating background information, the main elements of the story, and explaining peculiarities of the play and its performance. Sources, presumed author, and category of the play are also given, in addition to a wealth of notes explaining quotations and allusions in the text. Line drawings in the margins indicate costumes and poses of the major characters.

The plays are, in each volume, arranged in the order in which they would be performed; the stately god plays first, followed by the warrior pieces, wig or woman plays, miscellaneous pieces, and final plays. A number of well-known favorites are included such as *Sumidagawa, Funa Benkei, Kantan, Aoi no ue, Hagoromo,* and *Sotoba Komachi.* Some of the plays also exist in kabuki versions, although *Ataka* (known in kabuki as *Kanjinchō* or *The Subscription List*) is the only one whose kabuki adaptation has been translated into English (see no. **59**). Some of the plays exist in other English versions, and the student can profitably compare them: *Izutsu, Motomezuka, Momijigari, Yamamba, Matsukaze,* and others.

This collection offers a wide range of nō plays—such deeply spiritual and almost totally static works as *Takasago* and *Yuya* on the one hand, and such "dramatic" pieces as *Ataka* and *Funa Benkei* on the other. Plays with only two or three characters alternate with more complex works with as many as fifteen actors. A reading of these volumes will free the student from the usual clichés regarding the nō and give him an appreciation of the richness, variety, and complexity of this theatre which, on the surface, appears so simple.

33. Ueda Makoto, tr. and ed. *The Old Pine Tree and Other Noh Plays.* Paperbound. Lincoln, Nebraska; University of Nebraska Press, 1962. xxv, 63 pp.

This was the first book in English to present five nō plays in the sequence which would usually have been followed in the orthodox nō program, at least during the height of nō's development, when full-day programs were the rule. The author's introduction effectively sets the scene for an understanding of this sequence by first discussing the aesthetic theories of the greatest figure in nō history, Zeami. Turning then to the plays themselves, Professor Ueda deals with them particularly as a representation of man's spiritual adventure—the dramatist and actors leading the spectator to the experience of the "sublime" (Ueda's translation of *Yūgen,* a vague word with many meanings and variously translated by different writers). "The performance of five nō plays in orthodox sequence," the author claims, "thus delineates man in innocence, fall, repentance, redemption, and final glory." Whether all critics would agree with this analysis is dubious, but it offers a fruitful perspective from which to view the five plays offered in the volume.

The introductory or God Play, *The Old Pine Tree,* is, as tradition decrees, a stately, almost static, congratulatory piece in which gods appear to a traveller and perform a ritual dance. The Man Play (sometimes called Warrior Play), *The Battle of Yashima,* presents what many consider to be a typical nō structure: a travelling priest, arriving at Yashima, encounters two fishermen who tell him the story of the famed battle that took place there. They disappear and later one of them returns in his true identity as the famed warrior Yoshitsune and performs a dance depicting events of the battle of Yashima. The Woman Play, *The Woman within the Cypress Fence,* following the same pattern as the preceding play, shows a priest encountering an aged woman whose ghost subsequently dances for him and relates her sinful past as a court dancer, begging him to pray for her release from earthly bonds. *Jinen the Preacher* is the Frenzy Play. Actually this fourth group is miscellaneous and includes different kinds of plays, most of them cast in what, for nō, is a realistic mode: the action takes place as we witness it rather than being a recounting of past action by a ghost. Jinen reaches a boat in which slave traders have bound a young girl. He preaches at them, argues with them, and finally dances for them, and they free the girl. In the Demon Play, *The Mirror of Pine Forest,* a naive country girl looks into a mirror left her by her dead mother and thinks she sees her mother. When her father tells her the truth about the reflection, she prays for her mother, then falls asleep. In her dream, the ghost of her mother returns to her and dances until a guardian demon from hell comes to take her back; but, the daughter's prayers have freed the mother's soul, and the demon returns to hell alone.

Although all nō plays performed in the proper sequence might not bear out the innocence-fall-glory theory advanced by Ueda, the plays he has selected fit admirably into such a scheme. They are well-translated, beautiful plays which introduce the reader to the spiritual qualities which are certainly a most important dimension of the nō experience.

34. McKinnon, Richard N., tr. *Selected Plays of Kyōgen*. Paperbound. Tokyo: Uniprint, Inc., 1968. 123 pp. (Sponsored by the Japan Society, New York, and the University of Washington, Center of Asian Arts, Seattle).

Prepared on the occasion of the Nomura Kyōgen Troupe's tour of the United States, this anthology of ten plays is richly illustrated with photographs which add immeasurably to the reader's enjoyment, allowing him to form some idea of the spirit of fun which infuses these charming little comedies. A brief introduction presents a background to these comic interludes in the nō program which have, of late, become quite popular independently of the nō. Professor McKinnon stresses the comedy of situation, and the "delight in lifting the veil of pretension" which is visible in every kyōgen. Each play is preceded by a substantial commentary pointing up highlights of the work and its dramatic, comic, and aesthetic values.

Shrewish wives, foolish demons, self-important lords, clever servants, shrewd foxes—a whole array of animals, vegetables, and humans—inhabit these spirited pieces. In *Bōshibari* (Tied to a Pole), the master thinks he will prevent his servants from drinking his wine while he is away from home by tricking them into tying each other up, one with a pole across his shoulders and the other with hands behind the back. However, they outwit the absent master in the end by managing to help each other drink. *Tsurigitsune*, more serious and wistful than most kyōgen, shows a fox who assumes the guise of a priest in order to convince hunters to give up fox-killing. After succeeding in his efforts he is overcome with greed as he passes a fox-trap baited with a juicy young rat. In the end he barely escapes the hunter who, suspicious of the priest, has come to check the trap.

Two pages of kyōgen mask photographs are added at the end, their grotesque expressions suggesting the comic vitality of this theatre which exercises an immense appeal even in translation.

35. Keene, Donald, ed. *Twenty Plays of the Nō Theatre*. Tr. by Royall Tyler, et al. Records of Civilization: Sources and Studies, no. 85. New York: Columbia University Press, 1970. 336 pp. (Paperback).

The accuracy of these translations is suggested by the witty, and apt, dedication of the book, "to the memory of Etienne Dolet, burnt at the stake in 1546 for a mistranslation." Translated by students of Professor Keene, revised and re-revised time and again by translators, editor, and consulting poets, the versions in this volume are outstanding because they incorporate all the meanings and imagery of the originals without losing readability or poetic effectiveness.

An introduction by Keene outlines some of the major conventions of nō drama, both in text and presentation, stressing the freedom permitted the nō writer with regard to time and space. He points out the importance of atmosphere rather than character, and of the musical effect of the play's structure, which moves through three traditional sections: *jo* (introduction), *ha* (development), and *kyū* (climax). Describing some of the difficulties of nō scholarship, Keene traces the various ways in which authorship of plays has been hypothesized. At the same time, he acquaints the reader with the styles attached to the texts of authors writing at various periods during nō's development. One of the original contributions of this anthology is its organization of plays according to attributed author and in chronological order, so that the reader can note the evolution of the nō style, through the haunting poetic quality of Zeami's plays to the relatively realistic feeling of a late work like *The Bird-scaring Boat (Torioi-bune)*.

Each play is preceded by a brief note describing its themes, peculiarities, and origins. The text itself is supplemented with plentiful notes explaining allusions, and is decorated in the margins with line drawings of actors and props in major moments of the play. The plays, many here translated for the first time, and all of them benefitting from the most recent nō scholarship, cover a vast range of types from the almost totally static *Komachi at Sekidera* (considered so difficult and highly spiritual a play that it has rarely been performed in this century) to the dramatic *Dōjōji,* with its vengeful demon leaping suddenly into the temple bell; from the dazzlingly poetic *Deserted Crone (Obasute)* to the relatively prosaic *Bird-scaring Boat.*

While all of the plays are interesting in themselves, some worthwhile comparisons can be made with other translations or adaptations. *Lady Han (Hanjo)* is also one of Mishima's modern nō plays (no. 71), *Dōjōji* is the source for the famous kabuki dance play, (no. 61), and *The Valley Rite (Tanikō,* only partly translated by Waley in no. 30) inspired the modern German playwright Brecht to write his two short didactic pieces, *He Who Says Yes* and *He Who Says No.*

This superlative collection will remain for a long time the most authoritative and representative selection of nō plays within a single volume.

Kabuki and Bunraku: Criticism

(See also nos. **1, 2, 3, 6,** *and* **8–10**.*)*

36. Kincaid, Zoe. *Kabuki: The Popular Stage of Japan.* (1925). New York: Benjamin Blom, 1965. 385 pp.

This thick volume, the first devoted exclusively to kabuki, reflects an intimate knowledge on the part of its author. She successfully evokes for the modern reader the exciting atmosphere of prewar kabuki when many of the Western aspects of theatre-structure had not yet come to be accepted. Following an order which is somewhat arbitrary, the author first briefly compares Japanese theatre to Western, and then describes the kabuki audiences, its stage scenery and props, stage conventions, training methods, and ceremonials. In a second section, she relates kabuki's history, with ample illustrations. In the section on "Yakusha" (actors), she discusses in ingratiating detail the major actors of all periods of kabuki, relating picturesque or interesting anecdotes and mentioning the influence of the puppet theatre on the human actor's technique. In later chapters, theatre life is vividly evoked, and relations between society, the government, and the actors are treated. Music is discussed at some length, and the structure of the kabuki stage is traced through various epochs in its development. A section devoted to the playwrights of kabuki includes lengthy discussions of major writers like Chikamatsu and Namboku. Play forms are treated, with representative plays described in detail, as well as with examples of the major themes found in kabuki theatre. The book ends with a chapter on kabuki in the Meiji period (1868–1912) and "today" which was, of course, in 1925.

Miss Kincaid writes in a lively style, and never strays far from precise examples and amusing anecdotic illustrations. Because of the early date of composition, this book presents some information which has been corrected by later scholarship. But because of its date also, it is a valuable document on kabuki as it was before the great postwar Westernization. It gives fascinating insights into the early development of actors who are onstage today, or who were the legendary actors of yesterday. There is no other work in English which gives so much information regarding the lives and accomplishments of the many famous actors who have graced the annals of kabuki for over two hundred years.

37. Miyake Shūtarō. *Kabuki Drama.* (1938). 8th ed. Tokyo: Japan Travel Bureau, 1961. 157 pp.

This unpretentious volume attempts to give the uninitiated some insight into the world of kabuki. Although more a series of notes and hints than a developed introduction to its subject, it contains many of the essential elements with which the viewer must be familiar if he is to appreciate a theatre so unlike Western drama. Major characteristics and techniques are described, including some of the standard kinds of scenes that appear in classical plays, such as stylized fighting, head inspection, and narrative dance. The various kinds of plays are characterized, and brief synopses are given of forty kabuki plays. Several color photos and a large number of black-and-white ones enhance the text.

38. Sakae Shioya. *Chūshingura: An Exposition.* (1940). 2d ed. Tokyo: Hokuseido Press, 1956. 236 pp.

This study of what is probably the most popular of all kabuki and puppet plays among the Japanese, is divided into two sections, the first concerned with historical facts and the second with the drama which derived from them. An introductory chapter includes a survey of various plays dealing with the *Chūshingura* story before Takeda Izumo and his two collaborators gave it classic form in 1748. Adopting a didactic and somewhat stuffy tone, the author warns the reader that he must know the historical facts in order to be able to separate fact from fiction and thereby appreciate the drama properly.

Most of the first half of the book is taken up with recounting the true story of Lord Asano's unjust death and its subsequent revenge by forty-seven of his loyal retainers. This account reads almost like a novel, and is embroidered with conversations and descriptions which give it life, color, and a certain sentimentality. The most valuable part of the book is the thirty-odd pages focusing on "The Spirit of the Samurai." The chapter describes the complex net of relationships and obligations existing in the world of the warrior in medieval Japan.

The second half is largely made up of a detailed synopsis of the play itself, act by act, with brief commentary. The reader with access to the text of the play (no. **63**) need spend no time on this section. The short final "Appreciation" is perhaps hasty and superficial in its evaluation of a masterpiece that is a perennial favorite for dramatic as well as thematic reasons.

Aside from the attractive color reproductions of four of Hiroshige's prints illustrating *Chūshingura*, the chief interest of this volume lies in its graphic presentation of the historical background to one of the three greatest history plays in the repertoire of kabuki and the puppet theatre.

39. Scott, Adolphe C. *The Kabuki Theatre of Japan*. London: George Allen and Unwin, 1955. 317 pp. (Paperback, Macmillan).

This is one of the standard texts on kabuki by a respected writer on Japanese puppets, the Chinese classical theatre, and various other phases of oriental theatre. The approach is largely historical and descriptive, and the material is developed in a clear and well-organized manner.

In an introductory chapter, Professor Scott briefly characterizes kabuki, comparing it to Chinese theatre, and then presents an outline of essential elements in the Japanese social structure and psychology that will aid the reader in understanding the popular theatre. The following three chapters give the historical development of kabuki, and descriptions of the nō and puppet theatres which contributed no small amount to the popular theatre.

A chapter on music excellently describes the instruments and their use, and the chapter on dance offers the best concise account of this complex subject in English. Dance schools and their relationships are discussed along with the development of diverse dance forms, which are clearly illustrated by examples. The famous dance play, *Dōjōji,* is given a particularly detailed treatment.

"Actor's Technique" is perhaps the kernel of the book. It deals at length with the many techniques—various kinds of movement, speech, makeup, costumes, wigs, props, sets— which make of kabuki the exciting total form of theatre that it is. A chapter on the actors describes role types, traces the line of the Ichikawa Danjūrō name, the most famous in kabuki history, and presents a useful biographical list of living actors (in 1953).

Two chapters, devoted to playwrights and plays, describe the different types and their development, and are accompanied by detailed synopses of six representative plays. The book ends with a brief record of the development of the physical playhouse and stage. Appended is a lengthy glossary of Japanese terms. Scott's book forms an excellent introduction, and is useful as a reference work as well.

40. Halford, Aubrey S., and Halford, Giovanna M. *The Kabuki Handbook.* Rutland, Vermont and Tokyo: Charles E. Tuttle Co., 1956. xxi, 487 pp. (Paperback).

This compact little volume, packed with information essential to the understanding of kabuki in performance, occupies a very special place among kabuki lovers. Essentially it is a series of plot summaries of the major plays in the repertoire—or at any rate in the repertoire when the Halfords were writing (old plays revived recently do not always figure in this book). The plot outlines are given in great detail, with reference to possible variations in performance and to historical or dramatic background of the action in the play itself. Explanations of various peculiarities which might not be understood by the newcomer are also added. Whether the theatre one attends in Japan offers an English language program (as do the Kabuki-za and the National Theatre) or not, the spectator is well-advised to carry his Halford, for its explanations will invariably be fuller and more comprehensible than those found in the official programs.

As valuable as the plot summaries, if not more so, is the second part of the book: seventy-three pages of notes arranged in alphabetical order deal with dozens of aspects of kabuki that appear puzzling to the beginner, from "Actors and Roles," to "Zōri-uchi (Striking with Footwear)." Here the reader will find the names of major actors and their families, with pictures of their crests and the proper "shop name" to shout during a performance; explanations for using particular kinds of curtains, costumes, fans, music, properties; background information on major historical or legendary characters, wars, families, and so forth. A storehouse of kabuki lore, *The Handbook* makes fascinating reading as such, but is also conveniently organized and well-indexed so that one can find the pertinent item when it is needed for rapid reference.

41. Ernst, Earle. *The Kabuki Theatre*. New York: Oxford University Press, 1956. xxiii, 296 pp. (Paperback, Grove Press).

Professor Ernst's superb study of the kabuki theatre in its many complex facets remains, after more than fifteen years, the definitive study of this theatre. In an introductory chapter he describes the historical and social background which fostered the beginnings of kabuki in the late sixteenth and early seventeenth centuries, evoking the rise of the townsmen class at about the time that Japan was closing its doors to the outside world. Relating the theatre to this society, he sets the analytical tone of his study by taking up the problem of theatrical realism and theatrical reality as embodied, the one in Western theatre, and the other in kabuki.

A study of the physical theatre in chapter two makes clear the deep seriousness of his approach: he traces in great detail and with careful precision the development of the stage from something resembling the nō stage to its present form. Diagrams, precise measurements, quotations from contemporary regulations, examination of the development of the *hanamichi* (bridge through the audience), stage machines, etc., give this study a comprehensiveness that is satisfying to the theatre practitioner in search of accurate information. Many of the developments are illustrated with carefully chosen photographs.

A fundamental chapter is "The Audience and its Attitudes." Here the author's perceptiveness is revealed in his analysis of the Japanese psychology as it is embodied in the Japanese arts and particularly in kabuki. The study of aesthetics is first based on specific examples and then moves on from the specific to the general. Here, as elsewhere, Ernst establishes meaningful comparisons with Western theatre more familiar to the reader. Brilliant chapters analyze the *hanamichi*, the elements of performance, the stage and the actor, deducing general laws and aesthetic principles. We learn such useful details as the strength of stage areas, the importance of linear or pyramidal blocking, the function of decor and its change, the reasons behind elements of the dance, the essential qualities of rhythm and design in kabuki movement and speech. A sensitive passage analyzes the use of time and draws meaningful conclusions as to its significance in movement and posing. In short, Ernst makes profound sense out of much that in other writers is either simply described or else dismissed as beautiful and exotic decoration.

The chapter devoted to the plays, far from being a tiresome telling of stories or a simple listing of themes, offers an analysis of the moral content of kabuki as it related to Japanese society, and contrasts this with the content of serious theatre in the West. Dominant emotions are studied, but Ernst goes on to attempt to say *why* such emotions dominate.

A final chapter treats Western inroads and the uncertain future of kabuki. Having been one of the officers responsible for the classical performances during the Occupation, Ernst gives a firsthand account of that period, shedding light, as always, on the broader meaning of those experiences.

A model of elegance, organization, clarity, pithiness and precision of detail, this work—descriptive, historical and analytic—is at once the introduction par excellence for kabuki and the necessary reference for anyone exploring it in depth or seeking specific details for use in production.

42. Hamamura Yonezo; Sugawara Takashi; Kinoshita Junji; and Minami Hiroshi. *Kabuki*. Tr. by Takano Fumi. Tokyo: Kenkyūsha, 1956. 163 pp.

This interesting study of kabuki by four Japanese authors and critics has a concrete focus, plentiful examples, and an enthusiasm which prompted one of the authors to describe kabuki as "a flaming pillar of the most dazzling beauty, which is little less than the creation on earth of the nearest possible approach to a Paradise." The book opens with a visit to the kabuki theatre, evoking its lively atmosphere, and describing a performance of one of the supreme masterpieces, *Kumagai's Battle Camp*. The aesthetics of kabuki are described under the two major headings of pictorial and musical beauty, with reference both to *Kumagai* and to the colorful *Sukeroku*. An interesting comparison is made of varying styles in performances of the same plays.

The chapter on the plays themselves describes the development of types of drama and treats the conventions of obligatory scenes like head inspection, killings, and extortion. These are illustrated, as are many of the examples, by ample photographs at the beginning of the text. The remainder of the book treats the essentials of kabuki background and history, the actor's life and his roles. Perhaps its most original contribution lies in the sections that survey kabuki in the modern world. Reactions of the Russians during a tour in the 1920s and of the Americans during the Occupation are treated, as are the problems facing the traditional theatre as it adapts to the present. While the book offers no definitive answers, these great problems are given serious consideration.

This lively volume is a mixture of somewhat naive generalizations (due in part to the translation) and deep insights, offering much food for thought to the student in search of an understanding of this exciting theatre.

43. Scott, Adolphe C. *The Puppet Theatre of Japan*. Rutland, Vermont and Tokyo: Charles E. Tuttle Co., 1963. 173 pp.

The author of many books on both Chinese and Japanese theatre, Professor Scott begins his discussion of the Japanese puppet theatre by evoking the atmosphere today on Awaji Island where regional puppet performances still take place, and where, according to many authorities, the puppets originated. From there, he quite logically passes on to the puppets which have given most fame to the doll theatre in Japan, those of the theatres in Osaka. In the middle of the eighteenth century these puppets reached such a height of excellence and popularity that they outshone the living actors of the kabuki theatre, and the kabuki actors began to take over the plays of the puppet theatre in order to win back their audiences.

"The Masters of the Puppet" describes the work of the puppet manipulators, the narrator and the *shamisen* player, whose combined arts make up the fascinating and complex world of the bunraku as the puppet theatre is called, after the name of the man who revived the art at the beginning of the nineteenth century.

Three fast-moving chapters inspect the stage and theatre, the anatomy of the puppet, and the plays of the puppet theatre and include a discussion of some of the important peculiarities of Japanese life that are reflected in the plays and often prove perplexing to the foreigner.

A final chapter gives synopses of ten well-known puppet plays, representing history, domestic and dance style plays. The author also gives a detailed description of their performance on the bunraku stage, pointing out important visual and musical moments, an invaluable aid to the novice viewer.

While not termed a guide book, this small volume is of convenient size for pocket carrying and offers good introductory and explanatory material for the uninitiated spectator.

44. Malm, William P. *Nagauta: The Heart of Kabuki Music.* Rutland, Vermont and Tokyo: Charles E. Tuttle Co., 1963. xvi, 344 pp.

The outstanding authority on Japanese music here makes a

scholarly and detailed study of the *nagauta* music which is one of the basic musical forms used in kabuki theatre. The book is divided into four sections, the first of which is accessible to the beginner, while the remaining three are frequently, if not always, quite technical and will be more meaningful to the musician or ethnomusicologist than to the theatre amateur.

Part one presents the history and theory of the nagauta, arguing in convincing fashion that the *shamisen,* which accompanies it and is now the instrument par excellence of kabuki, was introduced into kabuki theatre some time before 1650. After describing the major ways nagauta is classified in Japan, the author discusses in some detail the formal structure of the music, comparing it with those of other important musical forms, and showing how they have exercised an influence on nagauta. Of particular interest for the theatre-oriented reader are the sections on *jōruri* (puppet narrative) form and kabuki dance form, which discuss lucidly matters that are usually ignored or only lightly touched upon in other studies of Japanese dance and puppet theatre.

Part two, "Music and Instruments," gives details on construction of the instruments and their use, as well as the melodies or rhythms which are played on them. The discussion here is quite technical and includes not only the shamisen, but the drums and flute as well.

Part three is made up of the careful and detailed analysis of two typical songs from the nagauta repertoire, *Tsuru-kame* and *Gorō Tokimune.* Since both pieces serve as accompaniments to well-known dances, this chapter, while not easy reading, is of immense interest to the dancer as well as the musician.

Part four, an insert in the back of the book, contains the Westernized musical notation of the two pieces just analyzed, with text in *rōmaji* (Roman letters) and Japanese, and several other musical transcriptions.

Although no doubt too technical for the beginner, this major contribution to the understanding of an important phase of Japanese music is a reference work of great value to anyone interested in exploring in depth the structure of dance which is so basic to all kabuki. For the layman, a careful study of the first part will be extremely enlightening.

45. Hironaga Shuzaburō. *Bunraku: Japan's Unique Puppet Theatre.* Rev. by D. Warren-Knott. Tokyo: Tokyo News Service, 1964. xx, 386 pp.

This useful volume might well have been called a guide to bunraku, for, like the guides to kyōgen and nō and the handbook on kabuki, most of its pages give plot summaries. Almost a hundred of the best-known puppet plays are sketched. While many of the plays are found in the kabuki repertoire as well, they are often performed differently, and sometimes acts deleted in kabuki are performed by the dolls, and vice versa. Hironaga's book is specifically adapted for the bunraku viewer and offers interesting comparisons with the kabuki versions as found in the Halford's *Kabuki Handbook* (no. **40**).

The synopses are preceded by two short chapters, the first of which describes the various elements that make up a puppet performance. The author rapidly discusses the relative importance of puppets and manipulators, the narrator, and the *shamisen,* and then explains the construction of the dolls, and particularly details the roles of the heads in the repertoire.

In the second chapter the author outlines the main steps in the development of the puppet theatre, including a wealth of detail regarding the chanters and the transformation of the style attached to the name Gidayū, which by the eighteenth century dominated other chanting styles in the puppet theatre. Hironaga describes the state of bunraku at the time the book was written, shortly before the founding of the National Theatre which today sponsors bunraku performances in Tokyo almost every other month.

Photographs in color and in black and white offer the reader views of the puppet heads (including a wide-eyed Ophelia for a 1956 production of *Hamlet)*, elements of the production, and scenes from puppet classics.

46. Saitō Seijirō; Yamaguchi Hiroichi; and Yoshinaga Takao. *Masterpieces of Japanese Puppetry: Sculptured Heads of the Bunraku Theater.* Tr. and adapted by Roy Andrew Miller. Rutland, Vermont and Tokyo: Charles E. Tuttle Co., 1958. 31 pp., 32 plates.

This large, handsome volume, as its name suggests, brings together photographs of the expressive puppet heads which are one of the forms of the Japanese wood carver's art. The interest of the book centers on thirty-two natural color photos of old heads, one to a page, each accompanied by an explanation and description of the roles for which it is used. Smaller black-and-white photographs show scenes from plays, the puppets "undressed," and an additional fifteen heads.

The eight pages of text serve to give the reader a vivid background of the Tokugawa period (1600–1868) during which the puppets developed and flourished, and to outline briefly the history of the bunraku (a word always used synonymously with puppet theatre) as it grew side by side with the kabuki theatre, both giving and taking from one another. Finally the authors trace the use of masks in several Japanese theatricals, contrasting them with the puppet heads.

For anyone interested in bunraku, this volume will offer a close-up view of many of the major types of heads which are striking for both their artistic and dramatic value.

47. Keene, Donald. *Bunraku: The Art of the Japanese Puppet Theatre.* Photographs by Kaneko Hiroshi. Tokyo: Kōdansha International, 1965. 293 pp.

The Japanese puppet theatre, often known simply as bunraku, is one of the three major theatrical forms of Japan, and probably the only theatre of dolls anywhere to be taken so seriously that it can boast a rich repertoire of dramatic and sometimes highly literary works. Professor Keene, with his usual clarity and depth, gives here the authoritative study of the bunraku, accompanied, as in the other volumes of the Kōdansha series, by a wealth of richly detailed photographs.

After evoking the exciting atmosphere of a puppet performance, the author points out the "pleasures of bunraku," which include, of course, observing the skillful integration of the three arts: puppet manipulation, *jōruri* narration, and *shamisen* accompaniment.

The development of these three elements is traced in a chapter devoted to the history of bunraku. The reader follows the growth of the puppets from crude ritualistic implements to the complex and sophisticated works of art they had become by the third decade of the eighteenth century. The dramatic and literary aspects in the narration slowly improved, until, having found the shamisen as its perfect companion, and having united the twin geniuses of the playwright Chikamatsu and the chanter Takemoto Gidayū, jōruri reached its heights in the early eighteenth century. Its immense popularity, its influence on kabuki, its gradual decline, and its present state are all chronicled in broad, clear lines.

In following chapters the various elements of the performance are described in detail, including the painful training for the different professions. The chanters, shamisen players, operators and their puppets, the texts, and gestures of the puppets are all discussed.

As always in the Kōdansha series, impressive photographs with full explicative captions form about three-quarters of the huge (10″ x 14″) volume. A few color shots showing full stage as well as detailed studies of several dolls are followed by about fifty pages of black-and-white pictures which give a dramatic idea of the impact of scenes from performances. Other pages have photographs of objects associated with the history of bunraku, regional forms of puppet theatre, chanters, shamisens and operators. Particularly enlightening are the several sections of photographs devoted to the gestural sequences in three scenes from famous plays. One scene is further illustrated by a recording, with accompanying text in Western notation at the end of the book—a magnificent addition for a theatre in which the music and voices are as important as the visual effects. Scenes from selected plays, a wide variety of puppet heads, properties, and stage sets round out the contents of the photographic section.

Appended to this superlative study are a list of plays, a chronology, and bibliography, always included in the useful Kōdansha editions. While this study is lucid enough to stand as an introduction for the novice, it is at the same time thorough enough to lead those already acquainted with bunraku to a deeper understanding of its background and aesthetics.

48. Shaver, Ruth M. *Kabuki Costume*. Rutland, Vermont and Tokyo: Charles E. Tuttle Co., 1966. 396 pp.

Although ostensibly treating kabuki costume, this book does a good deal more. The first section, about one-quarter of the book, traces kabuki from its simple beginnings, through the development of a highly sophisticated art form, and into the modern period. Writing for the general reader as much as for the specialist in search of specific information regarding costumes, Mrs. Shaver gives a clear and lively introduction to kabuki's long history, dividing it into the major era names used in Japan. While such a division may at first appear a hindrance, on the contrary, it not only adds color but helps to acquaint the reader with terms which he will come across time and again in his readings on Japanese theatre or history. There is great clarity of outline as the author tells her story with bold strokes of bright color, illustrating with picturesque or dramatic incidents, and pausing long enough to elucidate, where helpful, details of costume, wig, or props, typical of a particular actor or moment.

Part two, the bulk of the book, begins with a general survey of costumes in which kimono, *hakama* (divided skirt), and men's and women's clothing are briefly described. The following chapters carefully consider men's, then women's costumes, for *jidaimono* (history plays) and *sewamono* (domestic plays), armor, costume patterns and colors, crests, headbands, headgear, hand-towels, fans, swords, wigs, stylized makeup, ways of pulling up the kimono hem, quick changes onstage, and the costume department as it exists in kabuki today.

The chapters devoted specifically to costumes are divided into sections dealing with major kinds of costumes worn within each kind of play. Examples of characters who wear them are given, often along with historical information regarding development of the item, or its change within the kabuki traditions. Wigs and properties used with specific costumes are sometimes mentioned here as well. An essential part of the book is the large number of illustrations—over 250 in number, many of them in beautiful color. The watercolor drawings by Akira

Soma and Gako Ota, if sometimes not as dramatic or impressive as photographs might have been, are no doubt clearer in their indication of detail, and serve as illustrations of points made in the text.

Since no non-Japanese work examines kabuki wigs, it is particularly gratifying to find a discussion of that complex subject here. After describing the process of making the wig, the author treats summarily the main types of wigs, and supplements this with drawings of sixty-three examples and descriptions of them and their uses.

A useful glossary and bibliography are appended, as well as an index which, unfortunately, is inadequate.

Kabuki Costume is a pioneer work, an enormous undertaking which takes into account hundreds of costumes, wigs, props, and their variants for different characters, plays and periods. It is impossible to present any aspect of kabuki completely within a single volume, as the author admits in her introduction, and the reader will search in vain for reference to certain important plays or types of characters. He may experience difficulty too in finding what *is* there, because it is not always in the section where one might logically expect it. Nonetheless, even the beginner will find this book immensely helpful in his understanding of kabuki, for it is simple, lively and appealing; the specialist will find here helpful details which are available nowhere else in English, and not even in Japanese in so concentrated a form.

49. Dunn, Charles J. *The Early Japanese Puppet Drama.* London: Luzac and Co., 1966. 154 pp.

This scholarly book, best approached after reading some introductory work, delves into the period preceding the heyday of the puppet theatre in the late seventeenth and the eighteenth centuries. It is of immense value in understanding the various strands that contributed to the creation of one of the few truly serious and sophisticated puppet theatres in the world. In the beginning chapters, Professor Dunn studies early references to the story of Lady Jōruri, who was to give her name to the *jōruri* form, and he follows the development of the three elements—narration, *shamisen*, and puppets—which, in the late seventeenth century, combined to become the theatre which is today known as bunraku. In some detail he deals with the early story of *Lady Jōruri*, and with that other well-known early play, *Amida's Riven Breast*, but his treatment, scholarly and searching, does not make easy reading.

The central part of the book focuses on the puppets, theatres, and performers in the seventeenth century. The chapter entitled "The Chanters of Old Jōruri," is particularly interesting, for it comments on the types of plays that were being performed just about the time that the most famous of all Japanese dramatists, Chikamatsu Monzaemon, turned to the puppet theatre. The entire work is of great historical interest, and sets the scene most effectively for an understanding and appreciation of the contributions of Chikamatsu. It also offers insights into the theatrical world which was developing alongside the kabuki and influencing it already.

Thirteen pages of reproductions of old prints help the reader to grasp what is discussed in the text, while two valuable appendices offer translations of two old jōruri plays. The first, *Amida's Riven Breast*, is given on facing pages in a 1630 version and a 1660 version. The second, *Kimpira and the Goblin*, dating from the 1660s, is a spirited tale of the doughty warrior Kimpira (who inspired the first Danjūrō to invent his famous *aragoto* or roughhouse style).

While intended more for the specialist than the neophyte, if approached judiciously, this book has much to offer anyone interested in the development of both bunraku and kabuki.

50. Gunji Masakatsu. *Kabuki*. Tr. by John Bester. Photographs by Yoshida Chiaki. Tokyo and Palo Alto: Kōdansha International, 1969. 265 pp.

This handsome book of large dimensions (in every sense) answers at last the need for a work that gives detailed attention to the visual splendors of kabuki theatre and at the same time treats historical and aesthetic questions which can only be dealt with in a rich text. The author, Professor Gunji, probably knows more about kabuki than any other scholar in Japan, and with this text he has made available for the first time in English many of his discoveries, particularly regarding the early development of kabuki.

Because of their magnificent detail, gorgeous color, and significant organization, the photographs dazzle the reader from the start, but it is a mistake to overlook the brilliant text which, although occupying less than one-fifth of the book, contains some of the most revealing writing on kabuki to appear in the English language—and in a masterly translation that does not smack of translation. In the opening chapter, "The Spirit of Kabuki," the author contrasts this popular theatre with more aristocratic forms, and finds the spirit of kabuki in a "playful, fanciful, elaborately involved attitude," (*yatsushi* and *mitate*), as well as in the mastery of certain patterns or styles of acting (*kata*) presented within the framework of the "the two great mainstays of kabuki": the musical and pictorial elements.

The longest chapter traces the many vicissitudes of kabuki's long history with a rare clarity of outline and precision. Without attempting to cover everything in detail, Gunji stresses essentials, again including a number of points not available in English before. The remaining shorter chapters concentrate on skeletal discussions of the roles of the actor, the making of plays and the role of the playwright, elements of the production, theatre and stage structure, and the relations between actor and audience. Despite their brevity and somewhat summary character, these later chapters are replete with precise, important information, including many rare plums which merit careful study.

The photographs are logically organized and, unlike the other kabuki books, accompanied by intelligent and fully explicative texts. Forty-five large (10″ × 14″) pages, of which sixteen are in full color, present "Famous Stage Scenes" from a variety of plays in the kabuki repertoire. One page shows the famous entrance of Sukeroku on the *hanamichi* (runway through the audience) in a series of nine small photos, with accompanying explanation of the words, gestures and costume.

The following three sections of photographs are devoted to three well-known plays from the classic repertoire, and give a scene-by-scene account of the plays. Other sections show special techniques such as the climactic poses *(mie)* and exit dances *(roppō)*, stylized scenes, role types, makeup, properties, behind the scenes, sets, ceremonies and theatres, historical aspects of kabuki, and regional folk varieties. In short, this is the most complete and well-presented pictorial display of kabuki, accompanied by a lucid and compelling text.

Useful appendices include a list of plays mentioned in the text, a chronology of kabuki history, a bibliography, and perhaps most interesting of all (because unavailable elsewhere in English), a chronology of famous kabuki actors.

51. Dunn, Charles J., and Torigoe Bunzō, eds. and trs. *The Actor's Analects (Yakusha Rongo).* Tokyo: University of Tokyo Press, 1969. 197 pp. in English, 198 pp. in Japanese.

The Actor's Analects is a translation of the *Yakusha Rongo*, a collection of seven short writings about kabuki published in the late eighteenth century. The writings (divided into a number of brief notes) derive from an earlier date and are made up of the reported words of important kabuki actors of an early period in kabuki's history, roughly between 1650 and 1750. As such, they reflect what some critics would call true kabuki, that is to say, kabuki before the influence of the puppets became so strong.

An introduction by the editors traces briefly the history of kabuki, then discusses the different Japanese editions of the *Analects*. Finally, it explains various aspects of the structure within the kabuki world in the Genroku era (loosely, 1688–1720, the period when most of the actors mentioned in the *Analects* flourished), and makes a brief comparison of Genroku acting with Western acting today.

The editors have avoided any detailed discussion of the essays themselves, leaving the reader free to draw his own conclusions. At the end of each item, however, there are comments by the editors which attempt to clear up ambiguities in the text and to elucidate difficult allusions. The writings are

1. *One Hundred Items on the Stage.* Despite the title, there are only seven items. This piece, which gives advice and guidance to actors, is attributed to Sugi Kuhe, who was perhaps a teacher of the great actor, Sakata Tōjūrō.
2. *Mirror for Actors.* Stories of several primitive kabuki plays (pre-Genroku period) and historical anecdotes pertinent to kabuki and its performances.
3. *The Words of Ayame.* The most famous piece in the volume, it reports the words of the first great *onnagata* (player of female roles), considered by many to have been the greatest of all onnagata. The words found here are the basis for many of the beliefs still cherished today and continue to be studied by actors of the present.
4. *Dust in the Ears.* Advice and attitudes of Sakata Tōjūrō, the greatest actor of the period in the Kyoto–Osaka area, famed particularly for his playing of handsome young lovers.
5. *Sequel to Dust in the Ears.* Anecdotes about various actors, and their advice.
6. *The Kengai Collection.* More anecdotes regarding Sakata Tōjūrō.
7. *Sadoshima's Diary.* A prominent actor and dancer talks about the actor's life during his era and, in a final section, discusses *The Secret Tradition of Kabuki Dance.*

There are two very useful appendices: a glossary of technical terms, and a list of actors and others mentioned in *The Analects*, illustrated with quaint details of individual figures from old block prints.

Both scholarly and lively, *The Actor's Analects* is invaluable in gaining a graphic sense of this early, vital era of Kabuki. The notes and comments of the editors help clear up difficulties and point out interesting contrasts with present-day kabuki. The last half of the book contains the original Japanese text.

52. Andō Tsuruo. *Bunraku: The Puppet Theatre.* Tr. by Don Kenny. Performing Arts of Japan, no. 1. New York and Tokyo: Walker/Weatherhill, 1970. 222 pp.

This charming book, by an author who has known the puppet theatre since childhood (his father was a chanter), offers a lively introduction to the subject. Unlike most of the books on bunraku, this one does not treat the puppets, singers and *shamisen* artists separately and systematically. The author has chosen to present his subject in a historical perspective, which remains at the same time very personal and colorful; instead of abstracting, he has introduced the theatre in its many stages of development through the major figures who contributed to that development. At times it almost reads like a novel, particularly when Andō evokes the early life of Gorobei from Tennōji, a farmer who was to become the first great chanter, Gidayū. In partnership with the greatest dramatist of Japan, Chikamatsu, he was to raise the puppet theatre to its zenith.

Retaining a personal and highly individual tone, the author traces bunraku's history through its days of glory and into the nineteenth and twentieth centuries, always focusing his discussion on specific figures and theatres. Perhaps because of his personal involvement with the puppet theatre, Andō takes us most effectively into the theatre backstage and, beyond that, into the lives and minds of the artists. A final chapter on "The Meaning of Tradition" bears reading by anyone interested in any of the traditional Japanese arts, and might well be taken to heart by performers of all sorts.

Like the other volumes in this very attractive series, this one features a wealth of beautiful pictures in color and black and white. Through them the reader gains a vivid idea of the puppets and their history. The usual chronology and explanations of the illustrations add greatly to the value of this volume which, like the others, is skillfully translated by Don Kenny.

This book is unpretentious without being naive, and painlessly offers insights which are not to be found elsewhere in English.

53. Toita Yasuji. *Kabuki: The Popular Theatre*. Tr. by Don Kenny. Performing Arts of Japan, no. 2. New York, Tokyo and Kyoto: Weatherhill/Tankosha, 1970. 245 pp.

This beautifully illustrated book by one of Japan' better-known kabuki critics is crammed full of interesting information and anecdotes, given somewhat helter skelter. The introduction by Donald Keene presents a vivid appreciation of kabuki, stressing the dramatic impact of a performance and the major epochs in its development. The text proper, although divided into three chapters dealing with kabuki's idiosyncracies, its history, and its condition today, is in fact a series of disconnected notes. The author presents a good deal of information but it is not integrated into a carefully planned text.

The most interesting part of the text is the third chapter, on kabuki today, which treats summarily such relatively unknown aspects of this theatre as women's kabuki, production problems, and the National Theatre. A chronology of kabuki's development and explanatory captions for the photographs are placed at the end of the volume. Play names, given in English, are helpful to an understanding of the titles, but often are difficult to trace back to the original (and sometimes better-known) Japanese title.

The real glory of the volume lies in the photographs. Of the 245 pages, only 105 are text, and most of the rest are devoted to magnificent photographs, many of them in lavish color. Scenes from plays, and paintings and prints from early periods of kabuki, give the reader a vivid idea of the past and present of this exuberant theatre.

54. Toita Yasuji and Yoshida Chiaki. *Kabuki.* Tr. by Fred Dunbar. Hoikusha Color Books. Paperbound. Osaka: Hoikusha Publishing Co., 1970. 127 pp.

In a tiny (4" × 6") format this volume presents a series of pictures depicting kabuki as it is performed today. Each page is accompanied by descriptive text which explains the details of the photographs. First we enter the theatre, then witness an *onnagata* making up, followed by several scenes from the dance play, *Dōjōji.* Many scenes from famous plays are included, usually arranged thematically or according to the kinds of action taking place.

Every other page of this inexpensive book features photographs in dazzling colors, remarkably clear and detailed for

the small size. Alternating pages are in black and white. After
96 pages of photos, there are 30 pages of text describing various
aspects of the performance, actors, costumes, properties, and
such. While not pretending to be thorough, it gives some interesting details not found elsewhere, and usually bases its discussion on specific examples from plays. Professor Toita, one of
the most knowledgeable kabuki critics in Japan, expresses himself strongly in favor of a return to the authenticity of earlier
days, and a weeding out of undesirable mannerisms.

The translator of this volume bears an English name, but
the translation itself is not native English; it possesses a naive
and colorful tone which does not hinder understanding, and
actually adds a certain amusement to the reading. The chief
glory of the book, however, lies in its plentiful photographs.

55. Yoshida Chiaki. *Kabuki.* Japan Times Photo Book. Tokyo:
Japan Times, Ltd., 1971. 112 pp.

This attractive book of photographs is a fitting introduction
to a theatrical art that is overwhelming in its visual impact.
A simple, rather charmingly naive introduction sets the mood
of a kabuki performance. Black-and-white photos are followed
by an "Invitation to Kabuki," which, as its title implies, makes
no pretensions to completeness or scholarly depth. Instead, the
beginner is introduced to a number of the fascinating and
unusual aspects of kabuki performance and its history. But the
chief value of the book lies in its photos which are large, varied,
and clear (usually one photo to each 7" × 10" page). Captions
give a brief explanation of the pictures, which are organized
generically and chronologically. A first section shows scenes
from dances, and from plays that contain a good deal of dance.
Scenes from several *Jūhachiban* pieces (plays belonging to the
famous collection of favorites gathered together by the Ichikawa
family) follow. Next are pictures of famous *jidaimono* (history
play)—*Chūshingura, Ichinotani, Sembonzakura,* etc.—followed
finally by *sewamono* (domestic play) scenes. The brilliantly col-
ored photos at the center of the volume, picturing a variety
of plays, give the reader a good indication of kabuki makeup,
costumes, settings, and poses.

While the text is relatively unsophisticated, the photographs in this volume are immensely appealing: they serve as a dazzling introduction to kabuki and permit further study of details in its visual expression.

56. Kawatake Toshio. *A History of Japanese Theatre II: Bunraku and Kabuki.* Paperbound. Tokyo: Kokusai Bunka Shinkōkai, 1971. 103 pp.

This volume attempts to bring into perspective the two major performing arts of the Tokugawa period (1603–1868), kabuki and the puppet theatre, by comparing them with each other, and contrasting them with the more aristocratic forms like nō and *bugaku* which are typical of earlier periods. In a general introduction the author (one of the best-known kabuki scholars in Japan and grandson of the outstanding kabuki playwright of the nineteenth century) sets the social scene that gave birth to these popular forms of theatre, stressing both the "this-world humanism" of the townsmen who made up the audience, and the constant restraints imposed by the military rulers.

The remainder of the book is divided into two lengthy chapters. The first treats bunraku, its aesthetic values, composition, texts, and history. For the neophyte, Kawatake introduces many concrete examples from plays to illustrate his points. Kabuki, likewise, is treated from the perspectives of aesthetics, drama, and history. The various categories of kabuki plays are described, and typical works are listed.

This book reveals an intimate knowledge of Japanese theatre, and has a sound scholarly base. The tone is occasionally naive, perhaps because of the translation, and the author takes great pains to make constant analogies to Western forms of theatre —analogies that often reveal his scholarship more than they add to our understanding of Japanese theatre or its universality. Twenty-eight pages of photos help visualize references in the text.

Kabuki and Bunraku: Texts

(See also nos. **11–16.**)

57. Shively, Donald H. *The Love Suicide at Amijima: A Study of a Japanese Domestic Tragedy by Chikamatsu Monzaemon.* Harvard-Yenching Institute Monograph Series, 15. Cambridge, Massachusetts: Harvard University Press, 1953. 173 pp.

This edition and translation of one of Chikamatsu's masterpieces was the first in-depth study in English of a Japanese play, and as such it remains a model of scholarly approaches to these difficult texts. Unlike Donald Keene's version of the same play (in no. **60**), which is more recent and no doubt reads more smoothly, this version reflects more accurately the state of the Japanese text; all stage directions as delivered by the narrator have been retained, and additions of the translator are carefully bracketed. Pivot words, which have double meanings, one relating to the preceding words, and one to the following, are translated with the second meaning enclosed in parentheses. Unlike the original puppet text, the character who is speaking is indicated—an immense help to the reader unable to witness a performance.

The Love Suicide at Amijima belongs to the *sewamono* category, or domestic tragedy, which deals with the problems of the lives of commoners, and most often with the conflicts of *giri* (obligation) and *ninjō* (human feelings). The extremely popular double suicide theme was treated a number of times by Chikamatsu, but this play is considered the supreme example of the type. The good but weak-willed young hero Jihei, has both a wife and a geisha mistress who are willing to make incredible sacrifices and vie with each other in their attempts to repay obligations. The drama is sometimes moving, but often so remote from modern ways of thinking that we find it difficult to perceive the presence of any conflict. This remoteness, as Shively points out, is one of its virtues, for it allows us to see, in perhaps a somewhat idealized form, the values of the Japanese merchant class of the eighteenth century.

The text of the play, occupying less than a fifth of the book, reads quite easily despite its brackets and parentheses. Scholarly apparatus of great value fill the remaining four-fifths. A lucid and well-organized introduction places the theatre into the Osaka setting of its day. It describes the life of the pleasure quarters and the *jōruri* of Chikamatsu, and studies in some detail the content, style and textual history of *Ten no Amijima*. The text of the play is followed by copious notes that elucidate allusions, difficult words, stylistic peculiarities, and occupy about twice the space of the play itself. A list of Japanese characters for the Japanese and Chinese words, names, and titles in the text is appended, as is an index.

Well worth reading for the translation of the play, the introduction and notes are also invaluable in themselves to anyone interested in the development of the puppet drama.

58. Segawa Jokō III. *"Genyadana": A Japanese Kabuki Play.* Tr. by Adolphe C. Scott. Tokyo: Hokuseido Press, 1953. 52 pp.

59. Namiki Gohei III. *Kanjinchō: A Japanese Kabuki Play.* Tr. by Adolphe C. Scott. Tokyo: Hokuseido Press, 1953. 50 pp.

These two translations of well-known favorites from the kabuki repertoire offer plays of strongly contrasting types. "Genyadana," one act from a much longer play, belongs to the *sewamono* or play of common people's life. A young man of good family, Yosaburō, having been separated from his former sweetheart, whom he believes dead, has now fallen on evil days and goes with a companion to extract money from a wealthy woman. She turns out to be Otomi, the woman he once loved. There is, however, no sentimental reunion. Instead, Yosaburō takes the money offered him by Otomi's patron, and leaves. A kind of genre picture famous for several poses and highly rhythmical speeches, "Genyadana" tends toward realism.

Kanjinchō, a universally acknowledged masterpiece belonging to the famous *Eighteen Plays* of the Ichikawa family, tells how, by cleverness and self-sacrifice, the twelfth-century warrior-priest Benkei saves the life of his master, Yoshitsune. The story is presented in highly stylized dance-play fashion, deriving largely from the nō play *Ataka* (in no. **32**) upon which *Kanjinchō* is based.

Both plays are carefully translated and accompanied by a detailed description of the action, costumes, decor and other elements of production. Line drawings by the author help to visualize climactic moments. An introduction to each volume presents pertinent background information, and an appendix offers descriptions and drawings of the wigs used in performance.

This text of *Kanjinchō* is included in Anderson's anthology (see no. **14**); however, Anderson has not included either the appendix or the introduction and extremely helpful synopsis of the play with its explanation of actions and themes that are not readily understood by the non-Japanese.

60. Chikamatsu Monzaemon. *Major Plays of Chikamatsu*. Tr. and ed. by Donald Keene. Records of Civilization: Sources and Studies, no. 66. New York and London: Columbia University Press, 1961. xvii, 485 pp. (Paperback reprint of four plays, *Four Major Plays of Chikamatsu*, Columbia University Press, 1961, 220 pp.).

This leading American scholar of Japanese literature has here translated and annotated eleven plays by Japan's most famous dramatist, including a number that figure almost annually in the repertoire of the puppet and kabuki theatres. Ten of the plays belong to the group known as *sewamono* (domestic plays), while only one—Chikamatsu's most popular play—is a *jidaimono* (history play). Such an imbalance reflects faithfully the accepted critical judgements of Chikamatsu's output, and is further justified by considerations of translatability, length, and comprehensibility for the foreign reader.

In a lengthy introduction Professor Keene pithily presents the background necessary for a deepened understanding of the plays. It is an introduction that might be read with profit even by those not intending to go on to the plays, for it gives a picture of society, life, and the puppet theatre at an important moment in Japan's development. After a brief discussion of major themes and types important to the genre (double suicide, adultery, the weak-willed young hero), Keene explores the plays as literature and elucidates some of the mysteries of Japanese literary technique, so often unlike those that give "literary quality" to occidental texts. Equally puzzling perhaps, for the Westerner, is the concept of morality as expressed in the plays, particularly the important notions of *giri* (obligation) and *ninjō* (human feelings)—both of which are explained simply and clearly here. The author underlines, however, his belief that the plays can be appreciated as human documents even without the insights offered through the introduction.

The eminently readable translations bear out this assertion, for the experience of human suffering in the domestic plays, and the bravura heroism of *The Battles of Coxinga*, are powerfully conveyed through the texts. Notes explaining allusions, plays on words, and other literary devices are plentiful, but not annoying.

The moving simplicity and brevity of *The Love Suicides at Sonezaki* (1703), Chikamatsu's first domestic tragedy, and the first of a long line of double suicide plays, rises to a poetic and dramatic climax in the final act, where Keene's translation proves even to the English reader that Chikamatsu is the great poet the Japanese have claimed him to be.

The Drum of the Waves of Horikawa (1706) is a story of almost unwitting adultery and its inevitable punishment and revenge. In *Yosaku from Tamba* (1708) virtue is rewarded when Lady Shigenoi, out of a sense of duty, refuses to acknowledge her own son rather than shame the princess she serves. The heroic son and his father, a samurai who has become a horsedriver, are finally recognized and restored to their former positions.

Blending tragedy and comedy as these plays often do, *The Love Suicides in the Women's Temple* (1708) depicts a handsome young temple page who must choose between the woman he loves and the attentions of a senior priest. The woman in turn must choose between the page and her intended husband. In an amusing scene, she fondles her lover beside her in the dark, while from the other side her unwished-for bridegroom makes unwelcome advances to her.

The quandary of Chūbei in *The Courier for Hell* (1711), one of the most famous of the domestic plays, is typical: impoverished, he cannot afford to redeem his courtesan lover. When his enemy offers to buy her and marry her, Chūbei breaks the seal on money that had been entrusted to him, and throws it on the floor with a great show of bravado. Facing dishonor and punishment, he and Umegawa flee but are captured before they can kill themselves.

Gonza the Lancer (1717) takes up the adultery theme again, this time with an interesting psychological twist. *The Uprooted Pine (1718), The Girl from Hakata (1719),* and *The Love Suicides at Amijima* (1721) treat the lives of young merchant-class men and their courtesans, but each with a different stress. The first has a happy ending; the second takes us into the world of smugglers; and the third, often called Chikamatsu's masterpiece, presents the complex web of duty and human feelings among man, wife, and courtesan. *The Woman Killer and the Hell of Oil* (1721) is a gloomy murder story with a highly moral ending.

The history play, *The Battles of Coxinga* (1715), is a long, loosely constructed fantasy taking place partly in Japan, but mostly in a China imagined by a Japanese who had never been there. Ranging over seven years and including characters from all levels of society, even gods and animals, the play recounts the adventures of the young hero Coxinga as he restores China to its rightful ruler. Techniques invented to show off the possibilities of the puppets abound—grotesque caesarian operations, eyes ripped from the socket, a fight with a tiger. The breadth and vitality of the play are breathtaking.

Enlightening appendices—on prostitution in Chikamatsu's plays, and puppet performances of the works—terminate the volume. A paragon of dramatic translation and editing, *Major Plays of Chikamatsu* is the first volume to make apparent to the Western reader the genius of the man considered by the Japanese to be their greatest dramatist.

The paperback edition, *Four Major Plays of Chikamatsu*, contains the introduction and appendices of the original, and the texts of *The Love Suicides at Sonezaki*, *The Battles of Coxinga*, *The Uprooted Pine*, and *The Love Suicides at Amijima*.

61. Richie, Donald and Watanabe Miyoko, trs. *Six Kabuki Plays*. Paperbound. Tokyo: Hokuseido Press, 1963. 114 pp.

These translations were prepared for the tour of the kabuki in the United States in 1960. The plays contained in the small volume include all those performed, with the exception of *Kanjinchō*, and indicate the cutting that was done for the American audiences, not unlike cuts that are made in performances in Japan, depending upon actors, time, and other considerations. The stage directions for the performances in the United States are not given in detail but are sufficient to allow the reader to visualize the main outlines of the stage movement.

Each play is preceded by a brief synopsis. The texts include four relatively modern plays (1887 or later) and two old classics. Four scenes from the great history play, *Chūshingura*, cover the events leading up to and including the suicide of Lord Enya Hangan, the act which prompts the famous revenge of the forty-seven loyal retainers. The dance play, *Musume Dōjōji*, equally famous, is actually the lyrics to the song accompanying the various dances that the young woman performs in order to lull the attention of the acolytes at Dōjō Temple before she transforms herself into a demon and attacks the newly hung bell.

Kagotsurube (the name of a sword) is a tale of love and revenge in the brothel districts, most striking to the newcomer for its spectacular procession of the courtesan Yatsuhashi and her suite. *Tsubosaka Reigenki* (Miracle at Tsubosaka Temple) is the sentimental tale of an old couple saved from blindness and death by the mercy of a goddess. Written under the influence of Western realism, it offers little of the typical kabuki flavor. *Migawari Zazen* (The Zen Substitute) and *Takatsuki* are dance plays in the style of the kyōgen, or farces, which alternate with nō plays in the usual program and preserve much of the comedy and charm of those old works.

The plays are followed by an extremely interesting postscript that describes the reactions of the American public to the kabuki, and of the Japanese actors to the American audiences and to various exotica of American life. These notes and the texts themselves recall the important moment when the kabuki theatre made its first real contact with the American theatre public.

62. Kawatake Mokuami. *The Love of Izayoi and Seishin.* Tr. by Frank T. Motofuji. Rutland, Vermont and Tokyo: Charles E. Tuttle Co., 1966. 172 pp.

Kawatake Mokuami, the author of this *kizewamono* (raw domestic play), is considered by many to have been the greatest writer of kabuki plays in the nineteenth century. The wide variety of characters in this play—dwelling particularly on prostitutes and thieves, but including as well merchants of all kinds, priests and occasionally a samurai—is typical of most of Mokuami's well-known works, which, as in most kizewamono, depict the seedy side of life in a sometimes rough, sometimes sentimental manner.

This translation of *Izayoi and Seishin* is only a part of the total play, four acts out of the seven. The three missing acts deal with an entirely separate group of characters and are hardly related at all to the events we witness in these scenes, several of which have remained perennial favorites of kabuki audiences up to today.

The play relates the vicissitudes of Seishin, a weak-willed priest, too fond of women, who is cast out of his monastary for having loved a prostitute, Izayoi. Prompted by the more resolute woman, the young man agrees to die with her, and they jump into the nearby river. Izayoi is fished out of the water and becomes the concubine of a wealthy merchant who is in reality a thief. She finally leaves him in order to become a nun and pray for the soul of her dead lover. In the meantime, Seishin, too good a swimmer and too cowardly to die, accidentally kills a young page while trying to steal his money, and decides that fate has decreed he should embark on a career of crime.

Izayoi and Seishin meet again, and share together a life of

crime, rife with melodramatic incident. Finally, when Seishin discovers that the young page he had killed was Izayoi's young brother, he is overcome with remorse and the two of them commit suicide, thus giving the play a moral ending.

Professor Motofuji's interesting introduction discusses the life and times of Mokuami and points out important aspects of the play which, in this lively translation, takes the reader straight into the nineteenth-century low-life world so effectively portrayed by Mokuami.

63. Takeda Izumo II; Miyoshi Shōraku; and Namiki Senryū. *Chūshingura: The Treasury of Loyal Retainers.* Tr. by Donald Keene. Paperbound. New York and London: Columbia University Press, 1971. 183 pp.

This most popular play of the entire kabuki repertoire, traditionally performed every December, was originally written for the puppets. Of the many versions that have been created over the years, this is the one that continues to hold the stage and stand as a model against which any new versions must be measured. Today, in the kabuki theatre, the original text is performed with a number of changes. The text here translated with sensitivity and sharpness by Donald Keene is the original puppet version. It has the fortunate added feature of character-names appended to speeches, so that it can be read like a normal play script: in the original text, since narrative and speeches alike are all delivered by one singer, there is usually no precise indication of which character is speaking.

Professor Keene's introduction describes the historical events which gave rise to the story of the forty-seven *rōnin* (masterless samurai), and then treats the early versions of the play. In some detail he discusses the authorship of the present text written by Takeda Izumo II, Miyoshi Shōraku and Namiki Senryū who together also authored the two other plays which, along with *Chūshingura*, form the triumvirate of the finest history plays in the kabuki repertoire. (The other two plays are *House of Sugawara*, in no. **13**, and *Yoshitsune Sembonzakura* [Yoshitsune and the Thousand Cherry Trees], not yet translated.)

Style, characters and the major theme of loyalty are taken up next, and in the final pages Keene sums up the differences between the kabuki and puppet versions, and reminds us rightly that the popularity of *Chūshingura* points up an important aspect of Japanese culture—the colorful and violent—often forgotten by those who think only of the more austere Zen-related arts.

In its broad outlines, *Chūshingura* tells the story of the humiliation and suicide of Lord Enya Hangan and the subsequent revenge taken by his loyal forty-seven retainers who lull the watchfulness of the evil Lord Moronao, and finally, years later, attack his castle and kill him. Through eleven acts, which read quickly but play more slowly—the entire performance would take ten hours or more—the authors follow the unwelcome attentions of Moronao to Enya Hangan's wife (act 1), the determination of another young lord, Wakasanosuke, to kill the arrogant old man (act 2), and the insults of Moronao to Hangan which cause the latter to draw his sword and wound the villain in the palace of the shōgun's deputy (act 3). For this he is condemned to kill himself by ritual disembowelment, which he accomplishes just as his senior retainer, Yuranosuke, arrives in time to take the bloody sword from his master and accept his charge to avenge his death (act 4). The remainder of the play follows several of the retainers in their personal hopes and tragedies as they wait their opportunity to attack their enemy. The most famous of these are Kampei and Yuranosuke. The former attempts to raise money to contribute to the vendetta by selling his wife into bondage at a brothel (a common practice, at least in kabuki). Through a series of unfortunate coincidences, he becomes convinced that he has killed his own father-in-law, and he takes his own life; however, it is discovered in time that he is indeed innocent, and he dies happily in the knowledge that his contribution will allow his name to be added to the list of revengers of his lord (acts 5 and 6).

Yuranosuke, the head retainer, appears to have forgotten his master and dallies at a brothel teahouse. His behavior, of course, is only a mask to allay the suspicions of Moronao's men, and in act 7 he reveals his true intent and does away with one of the villain's chief henchmen.

The remainder of the play, infrequently performed, shows further examples of devotion and loyalty, and ends with the victorious attack of the loyal retainers.

This masterly version is the definitive translation of one of the most important works of Japanese dramatic literature, and offers the reader insights both into a dramatic masterpiece and into the psychology of eighteenth-century Japan.

Other Traditional Forms

(See also nos. 2, 6, 8, and 10.)

64. Malm, William P. *Japanese Music and Musical Instruments.*
Rutland, Vermont and Tokyo: Charles E. Tuttle Co., 1959.
299 pp.

With complete authority and clarity Professor Malm sets forth
for both the layman and the specialist the richness and complexity of music in Japan today. Benefitting from the latest methods
in ethnomusicology and from the author's thorough knowledge
of the Japanese language, this book presents both an overview
and a detailed study of the chief musical forms. It is the first
comprehensive study of Japanese music to be published in a
Western language for eighty years.

An introductory chapter sets musical achievements within
a historical framework. Then the author goes on to study religious music (both Buddhist and Shinto) and *gagaku,* the court
music of Japan. While these two chapters may seem unrelated
to theatre as such, the music they describe exercised a profound
influence on all subsequent music, including theatrical music.
Obliquely related to the major theatre forms are the music of
the *biwa* (a kind of lute), the *shakuhachi* (bamboo flute), and
the *koto* (sometimes described as the Japanese harp), as well
as various folk musical arts—each of which is treated in its
own chapter. Structure of the instrument, its history, musical
forms, and manner of playing are set forth in simple terms,
and amply illustrated in various kinds of notation, with drawings and photographs.

For the theatre lover, the longer chapters devoted to nō, the
shamisen (the chief instrument used in kabuki music), and
kabuki will be of particular interest. Here the reader will find
a brilliant discussion of the musical elements of the nō play,
which dictate the very structure of the work—an invaluable
aid in appreciating the play-texts that are available in translation
elsewhere, but do not always make clear the structural relevance
of the parts.

The chapter on the shamisen (a three-stringed vaguely banjo-like instrument) again offers valuable insights into such technicalities as its structure, tuning, and manner of playing, and distinguishes among the many kinds of shamisen music which are divided into two major branches: *katarimono* (narrative pieces) and *utaimono* (lyric pieces). The student of kabuki, reading this chapter and the one concerned specifically with kabuki, will be immeasurably enlightened regarding many of the mysterious sounds he has perhaps heard but never quite understood.

Extremely useful appendices include (1) a time chart of Japanese music history, (2) an outline of Japanese music notation systems, including transposition to Western notation of several examples, (3) advice on seeking out the hidden corners in Japan where one can hear concerts of Japanese music, (4) a list of recommended recordings, and (5) a selective annotated bibliography. The latter, like the well-organized index-glossary, includes the Japanese characters for important words, names and titles.

Lavishly illustrated with photographs, drawings and diagrams, beautifully printed and bound, this work is a model of scholarly writing, dealing in some depth with its subject while remaining accessible to the layman. (For an in-depth study of *nagauta*, the major shamisen lyric form, see no. 44.)

65. Garfias, Robert. *Gagaku: The Music and Dances of the Japanese Imperial Household.* Paperbound. New York: Theatre Arts Books, 1959. 34 pp.

This elegantly presented pamphlet served as a program during a visit of the musicians and dancers of the Japanese Imperial Household to the United States. The beautiful photographs and calligraphy and the succinct text make this an attractive and useful introduction to the ancient music and dance which, brought over from the Asian mainland in the eighth century, have persisted in an unbroken line in Japan until today, even though they have become extinct in their countries of origin.

Professor Garfias briefly relates the historical background of *gagaku* (lit., "elegant music") and the accompanying dance, *bugaku*, then undertakes an explanation of their formal structure, and the composition of the orchestra. The basic styles of dance, almost totally abstract and nontheatrical in their movements, are described, together with the costumes, properties and performing platform.

A section entitled "Gagaku Today" suggests the precarious existence of this eighth-century art form in the modern world, where it nevertheless possesses a certain vitality, for new dances are still created. The last part of the booklet gives descriptions of dances and musical pieces performed by the artists during their tour.

The content of this publication is much richer than its slim size would suggest. Gagaku is of immense interest in the history of Japanese theatre, for the rhythm of *jo* (introduction), *ha* (development) and *kyū* (finale) that underlies theatre aesthetics, originates with this ancient music and dance.

66. Araki, James T. *The Ballad-Drama of Medieval Japan*. Berkeley and Los Angeles: University of California Press, 1964. xvi, 289 pp.

This is a scholarly and detailed study of the *kōwaka*, a form of musical recitation accompanied by sparse movement which, among the warrior class of the sixteenth century, vied in popularity with the nō. For many years it was believed extinct, until in the early years of this century a living tradition of this performing art was discovered in a small village in southern Japan. Professor Araki examines the kōwaka both as a performing art and as a literary form. Since music plays a role in the performance, he treats technical aspects of the musical elements, comparing them to those in other old theatrical forms and studying possible influences. Indeed, this book offers a substantial descriptive history of the rich forms that made up the medieval performing arts of Japan: the classical *gagaku* of the Imperial court, the aristocratic masked and unmasked dances of *gigaku* and *bugaku*, Buddhist music, popular variety entertainments like *sangaku* and *sarugaku*, the refined nō drama, and various kinds of dances.

The section devoted to the literary aspects of the kōwaka describes narrative structure, descriptive techniques, and literary devices, with ample quotations in both verse and prose. Araki organizes the texts according to their themes, centering on the famous heroes Yoshitsune or the Soga brothers and the Gempei Wars, or treating miscellaneous subjects. He lists the extant works, along with a brief synopsis of each. Translations of two kōwaka texts are supplied, one in the narrative form as it was adapted for reading, and the other in the form in which it was used for performance.

An appendix treating the distinction between the two old popular entertainments, sangaku and sarugaku, valuable notes, bibliography, and glossary, are included. Many line drawings and musical transcriptions illustrate the book, amplifying the text and facilitating its understanding. A serious study intended primarily for advanced students, *The Ballad-Drama of Medieval Japan* gives many insights into the rich theatrical past of a country that has managed to keep many of its old treasures alive.

67. Ashihara Eiryo. *The Japanese Dance.* Tokyo: Japan Travel Bureau, 1964. 164 pp.

This highly informative volume contains the most thorough and systematic discussion of Japanese dance in English. Although the author, in his chapter on historical development, treats the many kinds of dance that still exist in Japan, his main focus is the kabuki dance, known in Japanese as *buyō*. The book opens with a brief history, touching on the ancient *bugaku*, and popular forms like *dengaku* and *sarugaku*, all of which contributed to the development of nō. Of course kabuki, is dealt with in some detail.

The most original portion of the work lies in the next two sections. In "The Essence of the Kabuki Dance," the author stresses the meanings underlying buyō gestures, and contrasts them with the abstractness of classical Western dance. Throughout the book he establishes comparisons and contrasts with ballet, which help to render more concrete the many valid generalizations he is able to make regarding Japanese dance. The three elements of dance, *odori, mai,* and *furi*, are distinguished, and something of the complexity surrounding their definitions is suggested.

The third chapter deals with the composition of kabuki dance plays, and describes the various parts into which a dance may be divided with comments on the style, rhythms and content typical of each. The remainder of the book takes up in rapid succession the dance stage, accessories, musical accompaniment, costumes, and uncostumed dancing. An appendix gives synopses of twelve popular dance dramas.

While the choice of vocabulary occasionally gives this work a naive ring, it is far from being naive, and will serve both the beginner and the more advanced student, particularly in its discussion of composition and aesthetic principles governing Japanese dance.

68. Kishibe Shigeo. *The Traditional Music of Japan.* Paperbound. Tokyo: Kokusai Bunka Shinkōkai, 1969. 57 pp.

It is not possible to write a detailed treatise on the varied forms of Japanese music in the space of fifty-seven pages, but this volume forms an excellent introduction to the subject (for more detail see the books of William P. Malm, nos. **44, 64**). Charts, maps, genealogical tables, drawings, and photographs of instruments and performers help elucidate the material in the book.

The volume opens with a rapid sketch of Japan's history and musical development, stressing the provenance of the instruments and the musical styles that were to become established as the traditional ones. A second chapter outlines the characteristics which distinguish Japanese music from many other kinds of music.

The major portion of the book is entitled "Outline of Eight Major Genres," and takes up, in chronological order, the traditional musical forms: *gagaku, shōmyō, biwa,* nō, *koto, shamisen, shakuhachi,* and folk music. For each, there is a brief historical treatment, a description of the performance, and an analysis of the tonal system and other musical technicalities. These are clearly illustrated with drawings of the instruments and examples of scales in Western notation.

Simply written, this book nonetheless demands a certain acquaintance with musical notation and vocabulary.

69. Gunji Masakatsu. *Buyō: The Classical Dance.* Tr. by Don Kenny. Performing Arts of Japan, no. 3. New York, Tokyo, and Kyoto: Weatherhill/Tankosha, 1970. 207 pp.

Professor Gunji is without doubt the most highly considered of all contemporary scholars of kabuki and Japanese dance. This study, presenting many facets hitherto unavailable in English, is historically oriented. The first section on the aesthetics of Japanese dance is necessarily slight due to the limited number of pages allotted to it. The second chapter, "Japanese Dance from Ancient to Early Modern Times," traces the long history of this form from the early religious dances, through the various medieval dances including nō, and finally into kabuki dance with all its many varieties and vicissitudes.

Perhaps the most interesting part is the last section, "Japanese Dance in the Twentieth Century." Recent developments, the New Dance Movement, and the importance and weaknesses of the Headmaster organization are pointed out.

In the brief space of forty-six pages the author manages to suggest the complexity and richness of Japanese dance and makes the reader aware of the many forms of dance that have contributed to what is today known as *Nihombuyō.* For the uninitiated, a section that describes more fully just what happens in a dance might have been helpful. Making up for this to some extent are the many beautiful photographs that are the hallmark of the Performing Arts of Japan series. Color and black-and-white shots depict scenes from dance plays, pure dance, folk performances, and studio rehearsals, and there are reproductions of old paintings and prints of early dances. The usual chronology and commentaries on the photographs greatly help in understanding the development of the art and details of performance.

A short introduction by Professor James Brandon gives a foreigner's view of Japanese dance, particularly as it is found in the kabuki theatre. Brandon, like Gunji, stresses the need for flexibility and imagination in the world of Japanese dance today.

70. Togi Masatarō. *Gagaku: Court Music and Dance.* Tr. by Don Kenny. Performing Arts of Japan, no. 5. New York, Tokyo and Kyoto: Weatherhill/Tankosha, 1971. 207 pp.

The author of this volume, a member of the *gagaku* orchestra of the Imperial Household, has adopted a very personal way of introducing the reader to the various phases of his art. He begins by describing his arrival at the gagaku theatre in the Imperial Palace grounds just before a performance. On his way through the building, he describes the stage and some of the instruments, costumes, and masks that are exhibited in glass cases. Conveniently, some of the spectators are clustered about the cases asking questions, and the author can then elucidate various points in the performance and its elements.

The text is divided into three sections, the first of which discusses the instruments, musical notation, masks and costumes, and touches on the music and dance. The second relates a brief history of gagaku, beginning with prehistoric Japanese music, through the introduction of music and dance from the Asian continent, to its blending with indigenous elements and its decline with the rise of the military rulers. The final section, "Gagaku in the Modern Age," describes its condition today; it points out that there is a revival of interest, and a number of orchestras aside from that in the Imperial Household.

Nowhere does the author treat the aesthetics and composition of gagaku music and dance, but Professor Malm makes up somewhat for this in his excellent introduction to this volume. He speaks of gagaku as illustrating "the chamber-music sound ideal," and analyzes its composition.

As with the other books in this series, the photographs (over 200) are of excellent quality, many in beautiful color. There are scenes from the dances, details of the masks and instruments, series of photos showing how several of the instruments are made, and samples of major poses. Performances in shrines and theatres, and shots of rehearsals (with an American student in evidence) are included, as are many pictures of historically important paintings, documents, masks and instruments. The chronology and comments on the photographs are very useful additions.

This book offers an adequate introduction to gagaku, but does not explore the subject in any depth.

Shingeki: Modern Theatre

71. Mishima Yukio. *Five Modern Nō Plays.* Tr. by Donald Keene. New York: Alfred A. Knopf, 1957. xxi, 198 pp.

Considered by many to have been the outstanding young postwar writer in Japan, Mishima Yukio is known in the West chiefly as a novelist. In Japan, however, he is equally famous as a playwright and has written both for the modern stage and the classical theatres. In *Five Modern Nō Plays* he blends the traditional themes and events of five of the most famous nō plays with Western modernity of form and realism of feeling. The plays are entirely contemporary in tone and, as Donald Keene points out in his excellent introduction, appeal even to those who do not normally care for the traditional forms of Japanese theatre.

Keene discusses briefly the structure of the traditional nō play, and compares Mishima's versions with the originals. In order to appreciate fully these modern works, the reader would do well to read the earlier plays, four of which are found in translations by Waley (in no. **30**), and one by Keene (in no. **35**).

Sotoba Komachi transforms the ancient poetess into a wrinkled old woman picking up cigarette butts in a city park. In *The Damask Drum*, the gardener hopelessly in love with a princess has become a janitor in an office building worshipping from afar a model in a dressmaking establishment. The modern protagonist of *Kantan* dreams, on his magic pillow, of big business instead of riches in China, and the ailing lady of *Lady Aoi* (represented in the nō play by a kimono spread on the floor) becomes a modern young lady, victim of sexual repression, in a psychiatric hospital. *Hanjo* replaces the happy ending of the madwoman restored to her wits by the return of her lover with a neurotic sinking into further madness as Hanako rejects the returned lover and remains with a possessive older woman who desires her.

An interesting view of new possibilities using old stories and themes, these five modern nō plays gain a good deal in easy comprehensibility, but lose much more in terms of poetry, depth, and universality. They remain, until now, however, one of the more successful attempts to create a modern Japanese theatre by combining traditional and Western modes.

72. Mishima Yukio. *Madame de Sade.* Tr. by Donald Keene. Paperbound. New York: Grove Press, Evergreen Books, 1967. 108 pp.

The *shingeki* (lit., "new theatre") of Japan, reflecting or rather imitating the modern Western theatre, is considered by most critics to have not yet reached a level of excellence. Among the few plays rendered into English, however, there are several by Mishima, generally recognized as the finest Japanese dramatist since the War. In a postface to *Madame de Sade,* the author describes the play as "Sade seen through women's eyes," and calls it an attempt to present a logical answer to the riddle posed by the actions of the real Madame de Sade: after remaining faithful to her husband during his long years of imprisonment, she left him when he was finally released.

In three acts, Mishima probes the attitudes of five women toward the man who has been imprisoned for his sexual excesses. Madame de Sade's mother, representing, according to Mishima, "law, society and morality," hates the man who has hurt her older daughter and attempts to keep him imprisoned permanently. Her younger daughter (representing "guilelessness and lack of principle,"), relishes the memory of days lived with Sade in Venice. Madame de Saint-Fond ("carnal desires"), is a kind of female de Sade, while Madame de Simiane represents religion. Against these one-dimensional antagonists, only the criminal's wife offers a portrait of complexity or ambiguity. Mishima's effort to bare the heart of this "devoted wife" results in some insights into the dark corners of the soul, and allows the author to indulge in descriptions of sensational sexuality.

In a passage reminiscent of Genet, but devoid of his violent lyricism, Madame de Sade accuses her frankly middle-class mother of knowing nothing "of nights when holiness and shame imperceptibly switch appearances." In a final apotheosis of the poet in de Sade, who through his writing has wrought creation out of destruction, the wife, now renouncing him and taking the veil, describes him as a kind of knight in shining armor. In contrast to this idealized picture is the brutal description of the fat, toothless pauper who stands vainly waiting outside the door as the curtain falls on the wife's refusal to see him ever again.

More dialogue than action, this play typifies the shingeki, which turns its back upon the superb theatricality offered by traditional Japanese drama. It is interesting for its ideas and characters, and as an example of the cosmopolitan outlook of young Japanese writers.

73. Endō Shūsaku. *The Golden Country.* Tr. by Francis Mathy. Paperbound. Rutland, Vermont and Tokyo: Charles E. Tuttle Co., 1970. 128 pp.

The film of Endō's novel, *Silence,* has rendered familiar the story that serves as the basis for this play as well. Based upon history, the play treats the question of a priest's apostasy during the persecutions that took place in seventeenth-century Japan. The head of the Bureau of Investigation in Nagasaki, Lord Inoue, had once been a Christian himself. Contrasted to the crafty and cruel Hirata, and the ingenuous young Gennosuke, Inoue is a man of heart and intelligence who has reached the conclusion that Christianity, whatever its virtues, is simply at odds with the Japanese temperament and character and will never flourish in what he calls "the swamp of Japan."

The plot of the play concerns Inoue's efforts to discover the hiding place of Father Ferreira, the last priest living in Japan, and when he finds him, his attempts to bring about the priest's apostasy. He finally succeeds in making the priest step upon the picture of Christ, one of the *fumi-e* (or "stepping pictures") that were used to test the religious inclinations of suspected Christians. Convinced that Christ understands and accepts human weakness, and hoping to save the farmers whose pastor he is, Ferreira denies his faith. Historically he became a member of the Bureau of Investigation and joined forces against the Christians, but Endō, with more charity than truth, does not follow him to this bitter end, and permits him certain attenuating circumstances that history does not record.

Dramatically the play pits the Christians against the persecuting pagans, much in the spirit of melodrama; scenes showing the virtue, fear, hesitation and faith of the former alternate with scenes revealing the cleverness, cruelty and perspicacity of the latter. But the drama's chief interest lies in its ideas, and particularly in the conflict between the hope of the Christians—Ferreira and Tomonaga (a samurai convert)—and the disillusionment of Inoue, who, at the play's end, seems to have won a moral victory, although the curtain-line announces the arrival of four more Christian priests under the cover of night.

An interesting introduction by the translator sets the historical background and contrasts the dramatic action imagined by Endō with what actually took place.

74. Abe Kōbō. *Friends.* Tr. by Donald Keene. Paperbound. New York: Grove Press, Evergreen Books, 1969. 94 pp.

Abe Kōbō is known in the United States chiefly for the film of his novel, *Woman in the Dunes.* His play, *Friends,* showing much of the intensity and concentration of that novel, is clearly influenced by the theatre of the absurd. An example of the modern Japanese theatre—aware of the most recent currents from abroad—it is written in a flat realistic prose that possesses none of the linguistic exuberance or inventiveness of a playwright like Ionesco. Like his plays, however, *Friends* attempts to create an atmosphere of oppression as the protagonist is gradually overcome by an inimical society.

Into the apartment of The Man enters a family of eight, insisting that they are his friends and have come to save him from loneliness. At first unbelieving, the young man can find no way to reason with them, to convince them that he truly prefers to be alone. Even the police he calls in to eject the intruders offer him no help. As the "friends" take over his apartment and his belongings, protesting their good intentions with cheerful callousness, the young man is reduced to pleading. Finally, bereft of job, fiancée, and even his health, he is shut up in a cage where at last he dies, a victim of helpers who had forced upon him their own views of love and social solidarity.

Like the author's novels, his play is a fable, but it lacks the rich exploration of character that the novel form permits, and possesses little of the subtle suggestivity or vital humor that give its European counterparts their deserved popularity.

75. Kitani Shigeo. *A Volcanic Island: The Sound of Night.* Tr. by Andrew T. Tsubaki. Paperbound. Tokyo: Teatro Co., 1971. 44 pp. in English, 43 pp. in Japanese.

This impressionistic one-act play belongs to the world of *shingeki* or new theatre influenced by techniques of the Western drama. While the author, as reported in Professor Tsubaki's perceptive notes, declares he was motivated to write the play because of "concern over the social condition of Japan," this motivation is not overwhelmingly apparent to the reader. However, it does become clear that, behind the poetic atmosphere and the human experience suggested through the seventeen short scenes, there are bitter memories of war.

The time is the present and the place, a small Japanese island in the Pacific. Three episodes are recounted, sometimes, as the notes point out, with recourse to the retrospective technique familiar in the classic nō theatre. Each episode, however, is fragmented, and the other two interwoven with it, thus building slowly and establishing a kind of rapport in sorrow among the characters portrayed. The first is an old man, the guard of a windmill that is to be torn down to make way for a missile power station. We glimpse very briefly the loss of his three sons who went off and were killed in distant wars. The haunting sound of the windmill underlies the scene, suggested by a chorus, "Battern, won! Battern, won!"

The second episode reveals a couple who run a store on the island. At first they mourn some mysterious loss, which is later revealed to be a baby son who, in Manchuria, was drowned by the mother in order to prevent its cries from bringing pursuing soldiers to the hiding place of the fleeing Japanese. The sound of bubbles, "pkn, pkopiko, pkn, pkopiko," accompanying the scene, takes on sinister meaning as we discover the past of the couple.

In the third episode, an old woman, while awaiting the return of her son from a fishing vessel lost in a storm, recalls the past to her granddaughter. She evokes the men she knew when young, who all went away to be killed in wars, and now lie buried under the shifting sand on the hill outside, "Saran, s, s-sa!"

Further Readings

Critical Reading on the Theatre

A number of chapters from books or articles from scholarly journals contain important contributions to an understanding of various phases of Japanese theatre. The following are particularly recommended.

GENERAL

Hisamatsu Sen'ichi. *The Vocabulary of Japanese Literary Aesthetics.* Tokyo: Centre for East Asian Cultural Studies, 1963. (Especially chapter 3).

Keene, Donald. "Realism and Unreality in Japanese Drama." *Drama Survey* 3 (1964): 332–351.

Ueda Makoto. *Zeami, Bashō, Yeats, Pound: A Study in Japanese and English Poetics.* The Hague: Mouton and Co., 1965. (Chapter 1).

———. *Literary and Art Theories in Japan.* Cleveland, Ohio: The Press of Western Reserve University, 1967. (Chapters 4 and 12).

NŌ AND KYŌGEN

Zeami Motokiyo. "Jūroku bushū (Seami's Sixteen Treatises)." Tr. by W. Whitehouse and M. Shidehara. *Monumenta Nipponica* 4 (1941): 204–239, and 5 (1942): 180–214.

McKinnon, Richard N. "The Nō and Zeami." *Far Eastern Quarterly* 11 (1952): 355–361.

———. "Zeami on the Art of Training." *Harvard Journal of Asiatic Studies* 16 (1953): 200–225.

Zeami Motokiyo. "On Attaining the Stage of Yūgen," "On the One Mind Linking All Powers," "The Nine Stages of Nō in Order," and "The Book of the Way of the Highest Flower." Tr. by Donald Keene in *Sources of Japanese Tradition,* vol. 1, ed. by Tsunoda Ryūsaku, William Theodore de Bary, and Donald Keene. New York and London: Columbia University Press, 1958. (Chapter 14).

Kaula, David. "On Noh Drama." *The Tulane Drama Review* 5 (1960): 61–72.

Wells, Henry T. *The Classical Drama of the Orient.* Bombay: Asia Publishing House, 1964. (All of Part 2).

Stucki, Yasuko. "Yeats's Drama and the Nō: A Comparative Study in Dramatic Theories." *Modern Drama* 9 (1966): 101–122.

Teele, Roy E. "Comic Noh Essential in the Noh Theatre." *Literature East and West* 11 (1967): 350–360.

Kanze Hideo. "Noh: Business and Art (interview)" *The Drama Review* 15 (1971): 185–192.

Tsubaki, Andrew T. "Zeami and the Transition of the Concept of Yūgen." *The Journal of Aesthetics and Art Criticism* 30 (1971): 55–67.

Ortolani, Benito. "Zeami's Aesthetics of the Nō and Audience Participation." *Educational Theatre Journal* 24 (1972): 109–117.

KABUKI AND BUNRAKU

Shively, Donald H. "Bakufu versus Kabuki." *Harvard Journal of Asiatic Studies* 18 (1955): 326–356.

Leiter, Samuel L. "Four Interviews with Kabuki Actors." *Educational Theatre Journal* 18 (1966): 391–404.

Pronko, Leonard C. "Metamorphoses of a Play: Puppet, Kabuki and Western Versions of 'Miracle at Yaguchi Ferry.' " *Sangeet Natak* 4 (1967): 37–51.

Pauly, Herta. "Inside Kabuki: An Experience in Comparative Aesthetics." *Journal of Aesthetics and Art Criticism* 25 (1967): 293–304.

Pronko, Leonard C. "Oriental Theatre for the West: Problems of Authenticity and Communication." *Educational Theatre Journal* 20 (1968): 425–436.

Goodman, David. "Kabuki from the Outside: Interviews." *The Drama Review* 15 (1971): 175–184.

SHINGEKI

Kurahashi Takeshi. "Western Drama in Japan—the Japanese Shingeki Movement." *Japan Quarterly* 5 (1958): 178–185.

Ortolani Benito: "Shingeki: The Maturing New Drama of Japan." In *Studies in Japanese Culture*, ed. by J. Roggendorf. Tokyo: Sophia University Press, 1963.

————. "Fukuda Tsuneari: Modernization and Shingeki." In *Tradition and Modernization in Japanese Culture*, ed. by D. Shively. Princeton, N.J.: Princeton University Press, 1971.

Goodman, David. "New Japanese Theatre." *The Drama Review* 15 (1971): 154–168.

Concerned Theatre Japan. A journal of recent developments in Japanese theatre, published quarterly. Editor, David Goodman. Nishi Azabu 3–1–14, Minato-ku, Tokyo, Japan 106.

Texts of Plays

Brandon, James R., and Niwa Tamako, trs. *Kabuki Plays: Kanjinchō, The Zen Substitute.* Paperbound. New York and Hollywood: Samuel French, 1966, 88 pp. (A separate publication of the two kabuki plays from no. **15**).

Bowers, Faubion, tr. *Chūshingura, Momiji Gari, Kumagai Jinya,* and *Kagami Jishi.* In *Kabuki,* the program for the 1969 visit of the Grand Kabuki to the United States, presented by Pacific World Artists, New York. New York: Program Publishing Company (1472 Broadway), 1969.

Mishima Yukio. *Tropical Tree* (tragedy in 3 acts). Tr. by Kenneth Strong. *Japan Quarterly* 11 (1964): 174–210.

Texts and Studies Scheduled for Future Publication

The following volumes are being prepared for publication, some nearer completion than others. The reader is advised to watch for books by the authors listed since titles may be changed.

Brandon, James R. *Five Early Kabuki Plays.* Contains translations of five very important kabuki plays: *Sukeroku, Narukami Fudō*

Kitayama Zakura, Ichinotani Futaba Gunki, Kuruwa Bunshō, and *Sakura Hime Azuma Bunshō.*

Brandon, James R.; Malm, William P.; and Chively, Donald H. A volume (or two) containing translations of kabuki plays, and chapters on kabuki history, acting and music.

Jones, Stanleigh H., Jr., and Pronko, Leonard C. An anthology of three kabuki plays: *Narukami, Yaguchi no Watashi, Nagoya Sanza.*

Tsubaki, Andrew T., and Yang, Daniel S. P. *Drama of Asia: Traditional and Modern.* This volume will contain Indian, Chinese and Japanese sections. In the latter are a nō play, *Kiyotsune,* a kyōgen, *Dondarō,* two kabuki plays, *Ibaragi* and *Kagamiyama* (final scene), and three modern plays, *The Red Tunic, Twilight Crane,* and *Vanished at Dawn.*

Ortolani, Benito. *History of Japanese Theatre.*

Satō Shōzō. A Study of kabuki.

History and Culture

In exploring Japanese history and civilization, the books below are recommended. The student will find further indications for particular subjects in the bibliographies provided in these volumes.

A short excellent introduction:

Reischauer, Edwin O. *Japan, Past and Present.* (1946). 3d ed. New York: Alfred A. Knopf, 1964. 323 pp.

A "classic" work stressing Japan's culture:

Sansom, George B. *Japan: A Short Cultural History.* (1943). Rev. ed. New York: Appleton-Century-Crofts, 1962. 558 pp.

A collection of essays by various authorities:

Down, Ray F., ed. *Japan Yesterday and Today.* Paperbound. Toronto, New York, and London: Bantam Pathfinder Editions, 1970. 256 pp.

A detailed political history to 1868:

Sansom, George B. *A History of Japan.* 3 vols. Stanford Studies in the Civilizations of East Asia. Stanford, California: Stanford University Press, 1958–1963. 500, 442, and 258 pp.

A more personal introduction to the culture of Japan:

Maraini, Fosco. *Meeting with Japan.* Tr. by Eric Mosbacher. New York: Viking Press, 1959. 467 pp.

A standard introduction to Japanese art:

Warner, Langdon: *The Enduring Art of Japan.* Paperbound. New York and London: Grove Press, Evergreen Books, 1958. 113 pp. and 62 pp. illustrations.

Index

Authors, editors, translators, and titles given in each numbered entry are all presented below in a single alphabetic listing. Please note that the usefulness of this index is limited: persons and titles referred to in the body of the annotations and in the introduction are not indexed. Since this bibliography is arranged chronologically and by topical groupings, the incompleteness of the index, the general editor hopes, is justifiable.